ANTHOLOGY

— for —

MUSIC IN THE TWENTIETH AND TWENTY-FIRST CENTURIES

D0162212

Western Music in Context: A Norton History

Walter Frisch SERIES EDITOR

Music in the Medieval West, by Margot Fassler

Music in the Renaissance, by Richard Freedman

Music in the Baroque, by Wendy Heller

Music in the Eighteenth Century, by John Rice

Music in the Nineteenth Century, by Walter Frisch

Music in the Twentieth and Twenty-First Centuries, by Joseph Auner

ANTHOLOGY

— for —

MUSIC IN THE TWENTIETH AND TWENTY-FIRST CENTURIES

Joseph Auner

Tufts University

W. W. Norton & Company

NEW YORK • LONDON

W. W. Norton & Company has been independent since its founding in 1923, when William Warder Norton and Mary D. Herter Norton first published lectures delivered at the People's Institute, the adult education division of New York City's Cooper Union. The firm soon expanded its program beyond the Institute, publishing books by celebrated academics from America and abroad. By midcentury, the two major pillars of Norton's publishing program—trade books and college texts—were firmly established. In the 1950s, the Norton family transferred control of the company to its employees, and today—with a staff of four hundred and a comparable number of trade, college, and professional titles published each year—W. W. Norton & Company stands as the largest and oldest publishing house owned wholly by its employees.

Editor: Maribeth Payne
Associate Editor: Justin Hoffman
Editorial Assistant: Michael Fauver
Developmental Editor: Harry Haskell
Manuscript Editor: Courtney Hirschey
Project Editor: Jack Borrebach
Electronic Media Editor: Steve Hoge
Marketing Manager, Music: Amy Parkin
Production Manager: Ashley Horna
Photo Editor: Stephanie Romeo
Permissions Manager: Megan Jackson
Text Design: Jillian Burr
Composition: Jouve International—Brattleboro, VT
Manufacturing: Quad/Graphics—Fairfield, PA

W. W. Norton & Company, Inc., 500 Fifth Avenue, New York, NY 10110-0017
wwnorton.com
W. W. Norton & Company, Ltd., Castle House, 75/76 Wells Street, London W1T 3QT

2 3 4 5 6 7 8 9 0

CONTENTS

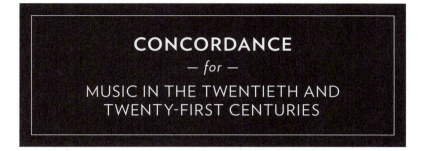

CONCORDANCE
— for —
MUSIC IN THE TWENTIETH AND TWENTY-FIRST CENTURIES

CHAPTER 7 | **The Search for Order and Balance**

CHAPTER 8 | **Inventing Traditions**

CHAPTER 9 | **Rebuilding amid the Ruins**

CHAPTER 10 | **Trajectories of Order and Chance**

CHAPTER 11 | **Electronic Music from the Cold War to the Computer Age**

CHAPTER 12 | **Texture, Timbre, Loops, and Layers**

CHAPTER 13 | **Histories Recollected and Remade**

CHAPTER 14 | **Minimalism and Its Repercussions**

This anthology is a companion to *Music in the Twentieth and Twenty-First Centuries*, the final volume in the series *Western Music in Context: A Norton History*. With its chronologically organized scores and analytical commentaries representing many major musical trends since the years around 1900, the anthology can be used on its own or in conjunction with *Music in the Twentieth and Twenty-First Centuries*.

The anthology compositions were chosen to provide moving, engaging, and challenging works that illustrate the central questions and issues explored in the book. Students will thus encounter both well-known and unfamiliar composers and pieces from 1896 to 2005, covering a wide range of genres, including symphony, tone poem, ballet, opera, solo keyboard music, concerto, choral music, and chamber music. Also represented are newer genres including radio art, music combining instruments and electronics, and a piece that questions the notion of genre altogether with its integration of music, dance, and ritual. The anthology selections are complemented by additional score excerpts in *Music in the Twentieth and Twenty-First Centuries* that further illustrate important composers and works, including pieces by Alma Mahler, Erik Satie, Darius Milhaud, Ruth Crawford Seeger, Colin McPhee, Ralph Vaughan Williams, John Cage, Lukas Foss, Libby Larsen, George Rochberg, Terry Riley, Arvo Pärt, and many others.

Of course no book or anthology of any size can do justice to the diversity of compositional trends over the last one hundred and thirteen years. This is particularly the case in recent years with the increasing globalization of our musical lives and the breaking down of borders between popular music, jazz, world music, musical theater, and sound art. Fortunately, during the same period the Internet has made it possible for composers and musicians to bring their works directly to a broad public; scores and recordings of many examples of the most recent trends we discuss are available online.

The analytical commentaries are intended to provide further pathways toward understanding the new ways of hearing and thinking about musical structure and sound discussed in *Music in the Twentieth and Twenty-First Centuries*. We will see composers questioning every aspect of what music is and what it might be, as made manifest in both their invention of new techniques and their incorporation of elements of the past or other musical traditions. We will consider works that can be understood in reference to explicitly articulated theories and systems, such as the twelve-tone method and its offshoots, as well as pieces that reflect more individualized solutions to the challenge of how to compose when anything is possible. New ideas about musical structure and performance have also necessitated innovative approaches to musical notation, particularly in works that include electronics, extended instrumental and vocal techniques, or very different ways of creating musical form. To facilitate analysis and classroom use of this anthology, piano reductions are used in some cases, but readers are encouraged to consult the full scores as well. I have presented poetic texts following the layout of their original versions, while also indicating alterations by the composers. All translations are my own unless otherwise indicated.

Just as compositional practice has become increasingly fractured and diverse, there is little consensus when it comes to the theory and analysis of the music considered here, including concerning fundamental issues such as the nature of tonality and post-tonality, the relevance of compositional techniques to the listener's experience of the work, and most importantly how we might understand musical structure in connection to its historical and cultural context. Readers should thus use these commentaries as starting points into the rich and often fractious scholarly and popular literature on these and many other works of the twentieth and twenty-first centuries.

A wide range of recording options gives students and instructors flexibility in listening to the music in this anthology. StudySpace, Norton's online resource for students, provides links to stream nearly every anthology selection from Naxos (accessible via an institutional or individual subscription), as well as links to purchase and download recordings from iTunes and Amazon.

I wish to thank my many colleagues who have commented on early drafts, and in particular my graduate assistants, Brendan Higgins, David Stallings, Monica Chieffo, and Kevin Laba. Special thanks to Justin Hoffman, Jack Borrebach, and Courtney Hirschey at W. W. Norton & Company for coordinating the production of this anthology.

ANTHOLOGY

— for —

MUSIC IN THE TWENTIETH AND
TWENTY-FIRST CENTURIES

GUSTAV MAHLER (1860–1911)

Symphony No. 3 in D Minor: Movement 4
Symphony, 1896

From Gustav Mahler, *Symphonies Nos. 3 and 4*. New York: Dover Publications, Inc.

50

TEXT	TRANSLATION	SECTION	MEASURES
		X	1–11
O Mensch!	O Man!	**A**	11–17
Gib Acht!	Take heed!	**B**	18–57
Was spricht die tiefe Mitternacht?	What says the deep midnight?		
Ich schlief! Ich schlief!	I slept! I slept!		
Aus tiefem Traum	From a deep dream		
bin ich erwacht!	I awoke!		
Die Welt ist tief!	The world is deep!		
Und tiefer, als der Tag gedacht!	And deeper than the day had thought!		
		C	57–74
		X′	74–83
(O Mensch!)	O Man!	**A′**	83–93
(Tief!)	Deep!	**B′**	94–99
Tief ist ihr Weh!	Deep is its woe!	**C′**	100–114
Lust–Lust tiefer noch als Herzeleid!	Joy–joy deeper still than heartache!		
Weh spricht, Vergeh!	Woe says, pass away!	**D**	115–129
Doch alle Lust will Ewigkeit!–,	But all joy wants eternity!–,		
–will tiefe, tiefe Ewigkeit.	–Wants deep, deep eternity.		
		X″	129–147

Mahler composed his Symphony No. 3 in D minor between 1893 and 1896; he conducted the premiere in 1902 and prepared a revised version in 1906. Lasting nearly two hours in performance, the six-movement work calls for a massive orchestra; the alto soloist from the fourth movement is joined in the fifth by a women's choir and a boys' choir.

Taken from Friedrich Nietzsche's *Also sprach Zarathustra* (Thus Spake Zarathustra, 1885), the text of the fourth movement presents the portentous words of the personified "Midnight," calling for mankind to affirm life in all its sorrows and joys. Mahler's setting begins with a slow and mysterious 11-measure passage (**X** in the table above) that evokes the tolling of midnight bells. He creates the static and timeless quality by destabilizing the meter through irregular groupings and by shifting the rhythmic placement of the alternating A♮ and B♮. On the second beat of measure 11, which corresponds to the start of the **A** section, the voice enters softly, intoning the words "O Mensch! O Mensch!" (O Man! O Man!). Mahler accompanies the repeated A♮s in the voice with tonally disassociated triads: F-major and A-minor; F♯-minor and A-minor. With his characteristically subtle orchestration, Mahler scores the two chords in each pair differently, the first with muted strings, the second adding muted horns and low harp.

The music at the conclusion of the **A** section (mm. 15–17) originally appeared in the corresponding measures of the symphony's first movement. This cyclical structure of the entire symphony finds a microcosm in the structure of the fourth movement: as indicated on the table, the mysterious **X** material returns in the middle and at the end.

The tonic of the movement is ostensibly D major, but this emerges only gradually and is continually challenged by D minor. The **X** music emphasizes A♮, while the first progression lands on F major in measure 17, a key that will return later in the movement. The **B** section (mm. 18–57) is based on a sustained D–A perfect fifth, but we don't hear a cadential progression in D major until the **C** section (mm. 61–67).

As in many of his works, Mahler uses the simple alternation of major and minor to great effect. He sets the words "Gib Acht!" (Take heed; mm. 20–23) with the pitches F♯ and E, thus suggesting D major. But on the word "Mitternacht" (midnight) at the end of the next line, there is a shift to minor with the appearance of F♮ (m. 32). He intensifies the major/minor alternation in the line "Die Welt ist tief!" (The world is deep; mm. 49–52), with the voice alternating between F♯ and F♮.

The C section introduces a more familiar tone, thanks to the expressive violin melody in measures 57–59, which also references music from the symphony's opening movement (appearing there in mm. 83–86). The melody's more regular phrase structure and rhythm are supported, as noted earlier, by the first functional harmonic progression in the movement, leading to a cadence on D major in measure 67. But two measures later there is a shift back to minor, followed by the return of the piercing oboe motif first heard in measures 32–35, which Mahler labels as "like a sound of nature." This sets up a transition to a variant of the cold and static X music.

Mahler begins the second stanza as a varied repetition of the first, starting with **A′** (mm. 83–93) and **B′** (mm. 94–99), which necessitated adding the lines "O Mensch!" and "Tief!" The **B′** section is interrupted by a sudden return of the warmer **C′** music, with the violin solo now in dialogue with the voice. By repeating the lines "Tief ist ihr Weh!" (Deep is its woe) and "Weh spricht, Vergeh!" (Woe implores, go) in the **C′** and **D** sections, Mahler creates more regular melodic phrase structures. These employ functional harmonic progressions, first arriving on F major in measure 112 and then returning to D major in measure 119.

But here again, at what seems like a moment of reconciliation or triumph, is a sudden reversion to minor with the "sound of nature" motif, and the movement begins to cycle back, as if inevitably, to the return of the dark and timeless X music. Yet the childlike joy to come in the fifth movement, with its boys' choir, ringing bells, and simple F-major folk song, makes it clear that the brooding fourth movement represents only one stage in the broad evolutionary development that Mahler's symphony charts.

CLAUDE DEBUSSY (1862–1918)

Estampes: Pagodes

Programmatic piano piece, 1903

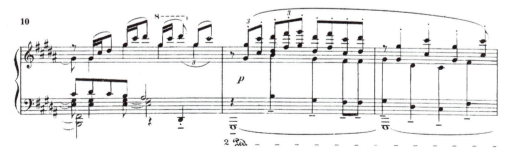

From Claude Debussy, *Estampes*. New York, Kalmus.

Animez un peu

Toujours animé

Revenez au **1° Tempo**

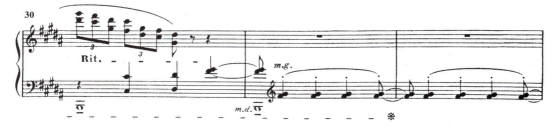

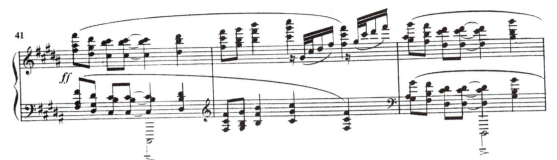

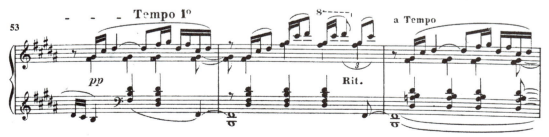

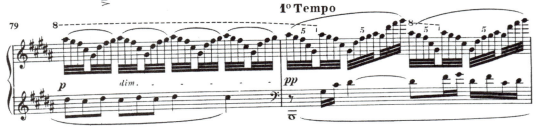

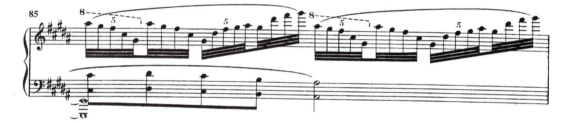

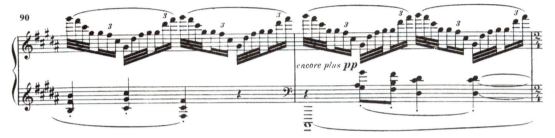

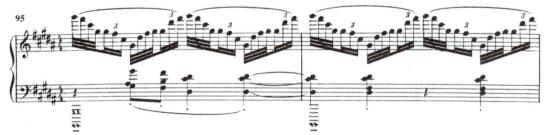

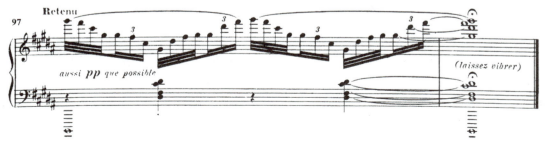

Pagodes (Pagodas) opens a set of three programmatic piano pieces Debussy published in 1903 as *Estampes* (Prints), referring to the Japanese woodblock prints then fashionable in Paris. Rather than depicting specific narratives, each movement captures a general scene and the feelings it evokes. The title *Pagodes* refers to the multitiered temples of Asia; the second movement, *La soirée dans Grenade* (Evening in Granada) is set in Spain; and the third movement, *Jardins sous la pluie* (Gardens in the Rain), depicts the French gardens of Debussy's childhood.

Pagodes is structured as **ABA′**, with each section mirroring this tripartite form. The piece begins in B major as if it will develop in traditional ways, starting with a progression from the tonic to V^7/IV (mm. 5–6) to IV^7 over a tonic pedal (mm. 7–9). A short contrasting passage (**b**, mm. 11–14) implies a movement to the relative minor, G♯, which is tonicized by a secondary dominant seventh D♯ in third inversion (mm. 15–18). Yet as the piece unfolds, the tonal elements dissolve into an overall sound world inspired by the structure of Javanese gamelan and defined by the pentatonic collection B–C♯–D♯–F♯, G♯. This pentachord, which contains both the B-major and G♯-minor triads emphasized in the opening, can be heard in almost every measure, supplemented in the various sections by E and A, and E♯ and A♯. Significantly, we never hear a dominant seventh in B major; instead, as in measures 20–23, Debussy returns to the tonic with a descending bass line: E–D♯–C♯–B.

Debussy incorporates many aspects of gamelan music: the low, sustained notes at the beginning evoke the large bronze gongs that are used to mark important formal divisions, while the fast-moving ostinato in the right hand (melody 1 in the chart on p. 24) represents the ornamented melodies played by the smaller bronze metallophones and wooden xylophones that comprise the core of the gamelan ensemble.

Imitating the gamelan technique of basing each piece around a *balungan* (melodic skeleton), Debussy in measures 7–8 (melody 2) brings in one of several slow-moving melodies in the middle register. With the exception of the diatonic melody 2, Debussy builds his melodies and many of the harmonies on the two main scales of Javanese music. The five-note *slendro* scale matches the basic pentachord of *Pagodes*: B–C♯–D♯–F♯–G♯. This is the source for the closely related melodies 3, 5, and 7. He uses a variant of this scale for melodies 1 (F♯–G♯–C♯–D♯) and 4 (F♯–G♯–A♯–C♯–D♯). In the **B** section starting at measure 33 (melody 6), Debussy adds to this an E♯ (resulting in E♯–F♯–G♯–B–C♯–D♯), bringing it closer to the seven-note *pelog* scale: E♯–F♯–G♯–A♯–C–C♯–D♯.

As noted earlier, *Pagodes* takes a traditional three-part **ABA′** form, defined by the varied repetition of measures 1–22 in measures 53–72. But due to the close relationship of the seven distinct melodies, the uniformity of the pitch structure, and the great variety of textures, the overall effect is closer to a theme and variations, or—as suggested by the title of the set—to paging through images of a scene viewed from different perspectives. This is especially true of the material identified as melody 1, which comes back in highly varied forms throughout the piece. We first hear it as a rapid pentatonic figure in the right hand (mm. 3–4) that sounds as if it will be the main melody. Instead, Debussy repeats the two-measure unit (mm. 5–6), then reinterprets it as an accompanimental ostinato (mm. 7–10). At the start of subsection **b** (mm. 11–14) he varies the rhythm and changes the second measure, while in subsection **a'** (mm. 23–26) he turns it into flowing arpeggios. Though not indicated in the diagram, we can also hear the figuration in measures 27–30, measures 45–49, and measures 78–97, as more distant variants.

SECTION	A						B					A'							
SUB-SECTION	a		b		a'		c		d	c'	a	b					a''		
MEASURE	1	7	11	15	19	23	27	31	37	45	53	57	61	65	69	73	80	84	88
MELODY	1	1+2	1+3	4	3	1	5	6	1+7	6	1	1+2	1+3	4	3	3	1	2	7

ARNOLD SCHOENBERG (1874–1951)

Pierrot lunaire, Op. 21: *Mondestrunken*

Melodrama cycle, 1912

From Arnold Schoenberg, *Pierrot lunaire*. Vienna: Universal Edition.

Den Wein, den man mit Augen trinkt,	The wine that one drinks with the eyes,
Gießt Nachts der Mond in Wogen nieder,	Pours down from the moon at night in
	waves,
Und eine Springflut überschwemmt	And a spring-flood overflows
Den stillen Horizont.	The still horizon.
Gelüste, schauerlich und süß,	Desires, terrible and sweet,
Durchschwimmen ohne Zahl die Fluten!	Swim beyond counting in the flood!
Den Wein, den man mit Augen trinkt,	The wine that one drinks with the eyes,
Gießt Nachts der Mond in Wogen nieder.	pours down from the moon at night in
	waves.
Der Dichter, den die Andacht treibt,	The poet, whom devotion drives,
Berauscht sich an dem heilgen Tranke,	Intoxicated by the sacred drink,
Gen Himmel wendet er verzückt	Turns his head enraptured toward heaven
Das Haupt und taumelnd saugt und schlürft er	And staggering, sucks and slurps
Den Wein, den man mit Augen trinkt.	The wine that one drinks with the eyes.

Commissioned by the singing actress Albertine Zehme, *Pierrot lunaire* (Moonstruck Pierrot) sets German translations of poems by the Belgian poet Albert Giraud depicting the fashionably decadent commedia dell'arte characters. The numerologically inclined Schoenberg organized the 21 movements of his Op. 21 into three groups of seven. After an extensive series of rehearsals, he and Zehme made a successful tour across Germany in the fall of 1912 that established *Pierrot* as one of Schoenberg's most influential works.

Inspired by the small, flexible ensembles of cabaret music, *Pierrot* employs a group of five players—piano, flute (doubling piccolo), clarinet (doubling bass clarinet), violin (doubling viola), and cello. The question of how best to perform the vocal technique of Sprechstimme (speaking voice), indicated by crosses on the note stems, has long been a topic of debate. In the preface to the score, Schoenberg instructs the vocalist to keep strictly to the notated rhythms, but instead of staying on the pitch as with singing, to immediately leave it by falling or rising to the next note in the melody. His score also specifies further gradations between singing and speaking; in measure 10, for example, the first two pitches are to be sung, while the next three are to be spoken.

The opening movement, "Mondestrunken" (Moondrunk), sets us adrift in a strange nighttime landscape, as the soft rays of moonlight swell into an intoxicating flood that sends Pierrot into inspired ecstasies. Schoenberg uses word-painting, with the delicate descending ostinato figures in the piano and violin and the ornamental flourishes in the flute providing a scintillating accompaniment to the voice. In keeping with the text, all these elements quickly begin to surge out of control, with ever more elaborate developments and layerings as the piece unfolds.

Like all the poems in Op. 21, the text of "Mondestrunken" is a rondeau of thirteen lines, with the first two returning as a refrain in lines 7 and 8, and as a truncated refrain in line 13. In several movements, Schoenberg matched the textual refrain with a musical return; other movements are through-composed. Here he repeats the music of the opening refrain (mm. 1–4) to coincide with the textual refrains in the poem in measures 25 and 39. He also uses the refrain music, together with the descending scalar passage in the piano's left hand in measures 5–6, to generate virtually everything in the intervening measures.

We can hear examples of Schoenberg's technique of developing variation in his treatment of the seven-note ostinato the piano plays in the first measure. After three exact repetitions, in measures 5–6 he interpolates other pitches to extend the figure to two measures; this version is then treated canonically, starting at the upbeat to measure 8. Much of the material that follows consists either of further developments of this ostinato (as in mm. 15–19, 25–31, 35–39) or of elaborations of the initial violin or cello figures.

As in other movements of *Pierrot lunaire*, some moments in "Mondestrunken" evoke elements of tonality, such as the isolated Bb-minor and B-minor triads in measures 23–24, or the emphasis on the pitch C—sometimes as the lowest note of the sonority C–F–B—in measures 7, 39, and especially in the climactic measures 29–33. But Schoenberg's " emancipation of the dissonance" is very much in evidence here, with the dense contrapuntal texture and the near-constant use of the complete chromatic collection.

In his later writings Schoenberg identified *Pierrot* as anticipating his techniques for integrating melody and harmony that would be so important to the development of the twelve-tone method in the 1920s. For example, the augmented triad, which first appears melodically in the piano ostinato in measure 1 (C–E–G♯), is stated as a chord in the right hand of the piano in measure 10 (D–F♯–Bb). In measures 26–27 Schoenberg transposes a four-note variant of the opening ostinato by major thirds, resulting in a large-scale unfolding of the augmented triad from measure 10 in the top voice (F♯–D– Bb–F♯). Yet such structural devices are less significant in their own right than as a way of giving voice to Pierrot's ecstatic, deranged, and inspired experience of the world.

ALBAN BERG (1885–1935)

Wozzeck: Act 3, Transition and Scene 3

Opera, 1922

*) H̄ bedeutet in dieser Szene Hauptrhythmus (siehe Takt 114-15)

) Die neuen Viertel (im Pianino und Gesang der Margret) sind gleich den Vierteln der vorigen Triole (= 120)

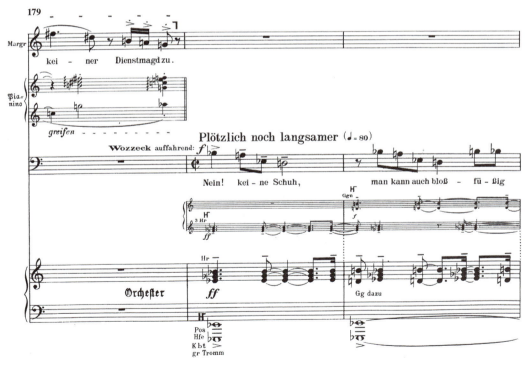

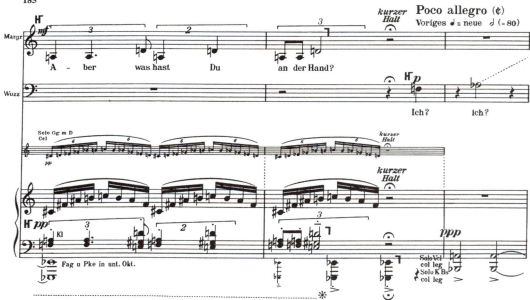

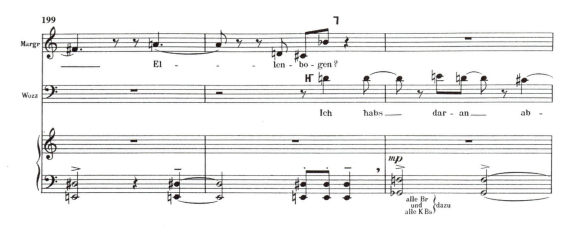

*) Sollten die Einsätze der Burschen und Dirnen auf unüberwindliche Intonationsschwierigkeiten stoßen, können sie vom Klavierspieler auf der Bühne – aber nur für die Sänger hörbar – angegeben werden.

*) *siehe Fußnote auf Seite 206*

*) siehe Fußnote auf Seite 206

A tavern. (Night, dimly lit).

Maids, among them Margret, and apprentices are dancing to a wild fast-polka.

WOZZECK *seated at a table*

Tanzt Alle; tanzt nur zu,	*Dance, all of you; just dance,*
springt, schwitzt und stinkt,	*Leap, sweat and stink,*
es holt Euch doch noch einmal der Teufel!	*One day it will take you to the devil!*

he gulps down a glass of wine (shouting over the piano player)

Es ritten drei Reiter wohl an den Rhein,	*Three riders rode along the Rhine,*
Bei einer Frau Wirtin da kehrten sie ein.	*They stopped by a madam innkeeper.*

the piano player tries to figure out an accompaniment for Wozzeck's song

Mein Wein ist gut, mein Bier is klar,	*My wine is good, my beer is clear,*
Mein Töchterlein liegt auf der——	*My little daughter lies on her——*

Wozzeck breaks off

Verdammt!	*Damn!*

and leaps up

Komm, Margret!	*Come, Margret!*

dances a few steps with Margret then suddenly stops

Komm setz Dich her, Margret!	*Come, sit down, Margret!*

he leads her to a table and pulls her on to his lap

Margret, Du bist so heiß . . .	*Margret, you're so hot . . .*

presses against her, then lets her go

Wart nur, wirst auch kalt werden!	*Just wait, you'll be cold, too!*
Kannst nicht singen?	*Can't you sing?*

MARGRET *sings while he listens*

In's Schwabenland, da mag ich nit,   *I won't go to Swabia,*
Und lange Kleider trag ich nit,   *And I won't wear long dresses,*
Denn lange Kleider, spitze Schuh,   *For long dresses and pointy shoes*
Die kommen keiner Dienstmagd zu.   *Aren't for servant girls.*

WOZZECK *raging*

Nein! keine Schuh,   *No! No shoes,*
man kann auch bloßfüßig in die Höll' geh'n! *You can also go barefooted to hell!*
Ich möcht heut raufen, raufen—   *I'd like to fight today, to fight—*

MARGRET

Aber was hast Du an der Hand?   *But what do you have on your hand?*

WOZZECK

Ich? ich?   *Me? Me?*

MARGRET

Rot! Blut!   *Red! Blood!*

WOZZECK

Blut? Blut?   *Blood? Blood?*

The others surround them

MARGRET

Freilich—Blut.   *Certainly—Blood.*

WOZZECK

Ich glaub', ich hab' mich geschnitten,   *I think I cut myself,*
da an der rechten Hand.   *here on my right hand.*

MARGRET *parodying his intonation*

Wie kommst denn zum Ellenbogen?   *Then how did it get up to your elbow?*

WOZZECK

Ich habs daran abgewischt.   *I wiped it off there.*

He leaps up

AN APPRENTICE

Mit der rechten Hand am rechten Arm?   *With the right hand on the right arm?*

MARGRET *and the others*

Puh! Da stinkt's nach Menschenblut!   *Phew! It stinks of human blood!*

WOZZECK

Was wollt Ihr? Was geht's Euch an?   *What do you want? What's it to you?*
Bin ich ein Mörder?   *Am I a murderer?*
Platz!   *Make way!*
oder es geht wer zum Teufel!   *or somebody's going to the devil!*

Quick curtain, as he rushes out

When Berg saw the 1914 premiere of the unfinished play *Woyzeck* by Georg Büchner, he knew at once that he wanted to make it into an opera. His service in the Austrian Army delayed most of the composition until 1917–1922; the first of many productions took place in Berlin in 1925. *Wozzeck* continues aspects of the Wagnerian operatic tradition, with a large orchestra and a close correlation between the stage action and the music based on an extensive set of leitmotives. Yet the opera also points to later trends with its Neoclassical formal features and diverse stylistic allusions.

The third scene of Act 3 takes place at night, in a tavern into which Wozzeck has fled after murdering his common-law wife, Marie, on a forest path by a pond. As in Expressionist art and theater, we experience the scene through Wozzeck's fractured senses, beginning with the distorted polka played onstage on an out-of-tune piano. Much of the harmonic language of *Wozzeck* is built on two dissonant hexachords, but Berg also employs more consonant triadic and polytonal harmonies. Tonal allusions are particularly important in passages evoking folk song and popular music, as in Marie's friend Margret's song (mm. 168–179) and the opening polka, whose disjointed triads mirror Wozzeck's erratic behavior.

Berg described Act 3 as a set of "inventions," which can be understood here as a kind of variation focusing on very limited material. The "Invention on a Note" in scene 2 culminates in two thundering crescendos on B in the orchestral transition between the second and third scenes. Here, we also hear pounded out in measures 114–115 the spasmodic rhythmic motive that will be the subject of the "Invention on a Rhythm" in the tavern scene. In the score Berg marks many of the appearances of the rhythmic motive with the *Haupstimme* (principal voice) symbol **H**, which he typically reserved for melodic lines.

Wozzeck's guilt, embodied in the rhythmic motive, permeates everything he hears over the course of the scene, starting with the opening polka, where the motive shapes the right-hand melody of the piano (mm. 122–125). It appears more subtly in diminution on the snare drum starting in measure 145, and then in augmentation in the piano (mm. 148–152) as the pianist struggles to find an accompaniment to the folk song Wozzeck sings. The leitmotivic significance of the rhythm is most explicit in measures 185–186, where Margret asks about the blood on Wozzeck's hand. Berg builds the nightmarish climax of the scene on seven statements of the rhythm starting low in the bass in measure 187, with each appearance getting higher and louder. More and more voices join in the accusations, most based on the rhythmic motive, until Wozzeck himself shouts out, "Bin ich ein Mörder?" (Am I a murderer?) and rushes back out to the moonlit pond.

As the curtain comes up at the end of the transition to scene 4 (m. 219), Berg introduces a pulsating six-note chord that sets the stage for the hexachord (Bb–C♯–E–G♯–Eb–F) that will be the focus of the "Invention on a Chord" used for Wozzeck's drowning scene that follows. With his characteristic attention to detail, Berg had already foreshadowed Wozzeck's death—as he wades further and further out into the pond to search for the knife and to attempt to wash away the blood stains—by using this hexachord in the *fortissimo* chord we heard in the transition to scene 3 on the downbeat of measure 114.

Ⓢ Norton Opera Sampler video available

Symphony No. 4: Movement 1

Symphony, ca. 1917

* [For example,] if six singers, three hum from "see," [m. 38,] [the men will take [the] words "Oh dost," [m. 37]); three others sing [the] words, hum[ming] only at [the] end.

Watchman, tell us of the night,
What its signs of promise are;
Trav'ler, o'er yon mountain's height,
See that Glory-beaming star!
Watchman, aught of joy or hope?
Trav'ler, Yes! it brings the day,
Promised day of Israel.
Dost thou see its beauteous ray?

Ives described the program of the first movement of his Fourth Symphony as "the searching questions of 'What?' and 'Why?' which the spirit of man asks of life." This sense of questioning starts almost immediately, when the bombastic opening fanfare in the piano, strings, and trumpet is interrupted to reveal the faint music of a small ensemble of four violins and harp that is placed apart from the rest of the orchestra. The melody they play is based on the hymn "Nearer, My God, to Thee" by the American composer Lowell Mason. But Ives undercuts the hymn's confident statement of faith with his scoring and dissonant harmonization, which make it sound distant and indistinct. For the rest of the movement this layer, which Ives labels the *Vox Angelica* (angelic voice, a soft organ stop), drifts in and out of audibility, its component parts out of sync with each other and with the main orchestra.

These first four measures introduce many other uncertainties, beginning with the key. The music of the main ensemble features a tension between D major and D minor, which continues throughout the piece as F♯ vies with E♯/F (see especially mm. 10–16 in the violins, and mm. 20, 29, and 40–41 in the piano). The *Vox Angelica* in turn has elements of A major and B minor. Ives's characteristically dense chromaticism also contributes to the tonal ambiguity by obscuring the triadic organization of the melodies and harmonies. Thus what could be heard as a dominant triad in the piano and strings on the fourth beat of measure 2 (A–C♯–E) is extended to include six other pitches (C–E♯–F–A♭–B♭–C♭), to which the *Vox Angelica* adds two more (D and F♯); only G is lacking to provide the complete chromatic collection.

Ives also causes us to question the formal function of the opening measures when a new, slightly faster section begins in measure 5, suggesting that measures 1–4 actually comprised an introduction. The main melody in the solo violin derives from the A-major tune of the hymn "Sweet By and By," but here again Ives weakens the conviction expressed in the hymn's text that we will someday rejoin our loved ones in heaven with a dissonant, out-of-kilter accompaniment in the piano that leads the melody chromatically astray.

That this main melody can be played by either cello or violin exemplifies the variability in performance that Ives allowed for in many of his works. Furthermore, Ives worked on the score for many years, developing related material in several other pieces. Although he composed much of the symphony between 1912 and 1917, he continued to work on it at least up to 1927, when the first two movements were performed at a concert in New York. Only the second movement was published in his lifetime.

We again have to question our interpretation of the form when the chorus enters in measure 17 with the hymn "Watchman" (also by Mason); now, everything that has come before sounds introductory. In "Watchman," a retelling by John Bowring of the Nativity of Christ, a watchman responds to the uncertainties of a traveler through the night by pointing to a bright star as a sign of the coming dawn.

Ives reorders the final lines of the hymn so that the movement ends on a question, "Dost thou see its beauteous ray?" Ives also reharmonizes the D-major melody with a somber accompaniment in B minor. He further complicates the texture by creating a dense collage of sound in this section, including whole-tone melodies (especially in m. 33), a quotation in the celesta part of the "Westminster Chimes" melody used in many church bells, and the ongoing chromatic material of the *Vox Angelica*.

The final G-major triad (blurred by an added seventh F and a C♯ in mm. 40–41) can be heard as either the subdominant of D major or the submediant of B minor; in either case, it is anything but conclusive. As the chorus fades into silence, Ives sustains the open-ended effect by interrupting the *Vox Angelica* in midstream. Only in the last three movements of the symphony does he begin to offer answers to "the questions of 'What?' and 'Why?'"

IGOR STRAVINSKY (1882–1971)

Le sacre du printemps: **Part I, Introduction**
Ballet, 1913

Based on a scenario by Stravinsky and the painter Nicolas Roerich, *Le sacre du printemps* (The Rite of Spring) was premiered in Paris by the Ballets Russes in 1913. The ballet begins with the curtain down, but from the opening measures of the score we are plunged into a Primitivist reimagining of springtime rituals in pagan Russia. Stravinsky characterized the Introduction to Part I as an experience of the immense and overwhelming forces unleashed by nature's renewal, anticipating the cathartic violence of the ballet's conclusion, where a young girl dances herself to death as a "consecration" of spring.

The very first sound in the ballet is the strained timbre of a solo bassoon at the top of its range. Throughout the Introduction Stravinsky features the many wind instruments from the massive orchestra, while avoiding the strings, which he claimed were too closely associated with the human voice and human expression. When the strings do appear in measure 20, they are playing pizzicato, waiting to use their bows until measure 34. After the curtain goes up in the next section, Stravinsky treats the strings almost as percussion instruments in the pounding chords of *Augurs of Spring*.

Stravinsky links melodic material to specific instrumental timbres. The opening melody is played by the bassoon each time it appears in the Introduction, just as the contrasting idea heard in measures 10–12 is usually associated with the English horn. Like many passages in *The Rite of Spring*, the bassoon melody is based on a folk tune taken from a 1900 collection of Lithuanian wedding songs.

Stravinsky distorts the tune's clear modal organization and triple meter, as if to submerge its more familiar human elements into the natural world's depersonalized processes of renewal. Crucial to this distortion is his use of octatonic melodic and harmonic structures, beginning with the collection C♯–D♯–E–F♯–G–A–B♭–C, the framing pitches of which can be heard in the major seventh between the c♯' in the horn and c″ in the bassoon (mm. 2–3). This version of the octatonic scale includes two minor tetrachords (the first four notes of a minor scale or the Dorian mode) separated by a tritone. Many of the folk-inspired melodies throughout the *Rite* emphasize this tetrachord, as in the English horn melody in measures 10–12 and the flute melody in measures 32–37.

Stravinsky's characteristic interaction of octatonic, chromatic, and diatonic elements is evident throughout the *Rite*. For example, the prominent B♮ in the bassoon melody in the opening measures does not fit in the octatonic scale given earlier. Yet the various individual voices tend to become enmeshed in the pervasive octatonicism, just as the modal B♮ in the bassoon melody yields to the octatonic B♭ in measures 4–5. The octatonic scale similarly permeates chromatic passages, as in the accompanimental bassoon lines in measures 14–19, with the lowest voices emphasizing F♯–D♯–C♯ from the lower octatonic tetrachord, or the piccolo clarinet figure in measures 21–24, which fills in the space between A♯ and E. The end of the Introduction, measures 52–65, combines many elements—the bright Dorian melodies in the piccolo clarinet and piccolo trumpet, a sustained second-inversion dominant seventh (B–E–G♯–D), chromatic lines, and minor tetrachords—but they are swallowed up in the overall mass of sound, here shaped by the octatonic collection B–C♯–D–E–F–G–A♭–B♭.

The Introduction largely dispenses with melodic or harmonic development. Stravinsky constructs it as a gradual accumulation of layers from a single voice to 30 different parts, a process he described in terms of buds bursting forth from an ancient tree, with each instrument becoming part of the imposing whole. As with the bassoon and English horn melodies, once material is introduced it continues with little change, often turning into an ostinato. Thus we hear the bassoon melody in measures 1–5, 6–9, 13, 42, and 44–45; the feeling that it is somehow always there in the background is confirmed when it suddenly emerges again out of the chaotic mass at the conclusion of the Introduction (mm. 66–68).

Stravinsky combines this process of gradual textural intensification with his technique of building forms by juxtaposing contrasting blocks of sound. In the opening measures the bassoon melody accumulates accompanimental voices (mm. 1–9) before being interrupted by three measures of the English horn melody (mm. 10–12). The latter is interrupted in turn by a new section dominated by incessant repetitions of D♯ in the oboe and chromatic figures in the piccolo clarinet (mm. 20–24).

But throughout this dramatic registral and textural expansion, Stravinsky avoids the impression of a series of small sections by building a sense of forward motion through his treatment of rhythm. He steadily increases the speed of the surface rhythms, as ever-faster figurations are introduced, while gradually clarifying and intensifying the pulse. After the flexible tempo of the opening (mm. 1–13), we first get a sense of a pulse with the accompanimental triplets in the English horn melody (mm. 14–19). This steady beat is reestablished in measures 32–37 and then intensified in measures 39–41 with the syncopated pizzicato C pedal in the solo cello. By the time we hear the B pedal in the double bass (mm. 57–65), the pulse has become an inexorable force, preparing us for the ostinato (mm. 69–70) that drives the next section.

7

KURT WEILL (1900–1950)

Der Lindberghflug, "Introduction of the Pilot"
Radio cantata, 1929

wa - ge es.

A (MM. 1—16)

Mein Name ist Charles Lindbergh.	*My name is Charles Lindbergh.*
Ich bin 25 Jahre alt.	*I am 25 years old.*
Mein Großvater war Schwede.	*My grandfather was Swedish.*
Ich bin Amerikaner.	*I am an American.*
Meinen Apparat hab ich selber ausgesucht.	*I selected my airplane myself.*
Er fliegt 210 Kilometer in der Stunde.	*It flies 210 kilometers per hour.*
Sein Name ist "Geist von Saint Louis."	*It's called the "Spirit of St. Louis."*

B (MM. 17—31)

Die Ryanflugzeugwerke in San Diego	*The Ryan airplane factory in San Diego*
Haben ihn gebaut in 60 Tagen. Ich war dabei	*built it in 60 days. I was there*
60 Tage, und 60 Tage habe ich	*for 60 days, and I spent 60 days*
In meine Karten meinen Flug eingezeichnet.	*charting my course on my maps.*

C (MM. 32—56)

Ich fliege allein.	*I fly alone.*
Statt eines Mannes nehme ich mehr Benzin mit.	*Instead of a person, I am bringing along more fuel.*
Ich fliege allein in einem Apparat ohne Radio.	*I fly alone in a machine without a radio.*
Ich fliege mit dem besten Kompaß,	*I fly with the best compass,*
3 Tage habe ich gewartet auf das Wetter	*I have waited three days due to the weather*
Aber die Berichte der Wetterwarten	*But the reports of forecasts*
Sind nicht gut und werden schlechter:	*Are not good and are getting worse:*
Nebel über den Küsten und Sturm über dem Meer	*Fog on the coasts and storms over the sea*
Aber jetzt warte ich nicht länger,	*But now I won't wait any longer,*
Jetzt steige ich auf	*Now I will take off.*
Ich wage es.	*I'll risk it.*

A′ (MM. 57—72)   INSTRUMENTAL

❧

Weill's music for *Der Lindberghflug* (Lindbergh's Flight) is set to a text by the poet and playwright Bertolt Brecht. The first version of the piece also included movements by Paul Hindemith, but these were later replaced by Weill's own compositions. In creating what they called a "radio play" or a "lesson for the radio," Weill and Brecht had to consider not only the aesthetic and political goals of producing a work that would be accessible to a broad audience, but also the technical limitations of radio broadcasts of the day, which included a restricted frequency range and considerable background noise.

The "Introduction of the Pilot" presents Charles Lindbergh's account of the preparations for his perilous solo flight across the Atlantic in 1927. Characteristic of the New Objectivity, the text is factual and direct, without any conventional poetic elements. This matter-of-fact quality is enhanced by the declamatory and syllabic vocal melody, which was designed to make the text more intelligible when the piece was broadcast. While there are some harmonic complexities, they are anchored by the strongly metric rhythms, regular phrase structure, and homophonic texture. The song's accessibility owes much to Weill's economy with the musical material; he derives most of the music from the two-bar unit introduced in measures 1–2, which can be heard in various forms throughout the piece.

As suggested by the tempo marking Moderato (Blues-Tempo), the "Introduction of the Pilot" is one of many works by Weill that evokes blues, jazz, and popular dance music. These elements can be heard in the syncopated melodic figures against the steady duple accompaniment, the regularly repeating two-bar bass line, and the blue notes in the melody (such as the F♯ in m. 9). Along with tenor, baritone, and bass soloists and a chorus, Weill's original score calls for a substantial orchestra, including strings; pairs of flutes, clarinets, bassoons, trumpets, and trombones; and timpani (not shown in the piano reduction). But his supple, jazzlike scoring, with prominent wind parts playing solo or in small groups, avoids the thick textures that would have become muddled over the radio.

The "Introduction of the Pilot" uses tonal harmonic material, including triads and seventh chords throughout, and perfect authentic cadences in the ostensible tonic of D minor (Weill provides no key signature). The harmony also alludes to jazz and the blues, emphasizing motion to the subdominant and progressions that move through cycles of perfect fifths. Much of the "Introduction of the Pilot" is based on the chord (B–D–F–A) that appears in measure 1. In some places, as in measures 19–20 in the **B** section, this can be heard as a half-diminished seventh, that is, the "Tristan" chord. But for the most part Weill treats it as the jazz harmony of a minor triad with added sixth (D–F–A–B). The **C** section, an extended vamp building up to the return of the **A** section, sends this added sixth chord through a cycle of fifths: B–E–A–D–G (mm. 32–43).

Weill uses functional harmonic progressions to define the main points of arrival; thus the cadences of the **A** (mm. 13–15) and **A'** (mm. 70–72) sections feature a German augmented sixth moving to a dominant seventh, then resolving to the tonic. Other passages, in contrast, rely more on subtle harmonic shifts that are connected through voice-leading by half or whole step. In measures 1–8, for example, the opening chord (D–F–A–B) travels to the subdominant G minor through a series of small alterations over the G pedal. Section **C** ends with the same kind of linear connections between harmonies in measures 44–55, which builds up to the forceful return of the opening of the work. This is now presented in purely instrumental form, as if to show us that Lindbergh is through talking and ready for action.

8

IGOR STRAVINSKY (1882–1971)

Symphonie de psaumes: Movement 2

Choral symphony, 1930

Expectans expectavi DOMINUM, et intendit mihi.	*I waited patiently for the Lord, and he inclined unto me, and heard my cry.*
Et exaudivit preces meas: et eduxit me de lacu miseriae, et de luto fæcis.	*He brought me up also out of a horrible pit, out of the miry clay.*
Et statuit super petram pedes meos: et direxit gressus meos.	*And set my feet upon the rock, and established my goings.*
Et immisit in os meum canticum novum, carmen DEO nostro. Videbunt multi, videbunt et timebunt: et sperabunt in DOMINO.	*And he hath put a new song in my mouth, even praise unto our God. Many shall see it, and fear: And shall trust in the Lord.*

When Stravinsky wrote the *Symphonie de psaumes* (Symphony of Psalms) in 1930, on commission for the Boston Symphony Orchestra, he had not composed a proper symphony since an early effort in E♭ from 1907. And not until 1940, with the Symphony in C, did he return to the genre in its traditional conception. In its nontraditional approach, the *Symphony of Psalms* is closer to his *Symphonies of Wind Instruments* (1920), where the title alludes to the literal meaning of the term *symphony* as "sounding together." Stravinsky's goal was to write a choral work in which the vocal and instrumental forces would be on equal footing; throughout the three continuous movements of the *Symphony of Psalms* he explores various ways of opposing and integrating the instruments and the mixed chorus (which, when possible, is to include children's voices in the sopranos and altos). The scoring shows Stravinsky's preference for what he regarded as the colder and less emotive sound of the wind instruments. While he does use cellos and basses, he replaces violins and violas with an expanded wind section.

Dedicated to "the Glory of God," the work is based on excerpts from the Latin Vulgate versions of Psalms. The second movement setting Psalm 39, verses 2–4, contains some text expression, particularly with the overall motion from the depths of despair at the opening to the spirit of thanksgiving at the conclusion. Yet while there are passages of luminous beauty, such as the end of the second and third movements, much of the work has an intentionally severe and stark tone in keeping with Stravinsky's interest in the ritualistic and formal aspects of religion.

The real focus of the second movement is Stravinsky's contrapuntal technique: an elaborate double fugue connects him to the tradition of sacred choral music and especially to J. S. Bach, whose *Musical Offering* is evoked by the opening subject. As shown in the following table, the movement begins with a

FORM	Fugue 1	Episode	Fugue 2	Episode	Stretto	Stretto	General pause	Episode
MEASURES	1–22	23–28	29–46	47–51	52–60	61–69	70	71–88
TEXT			Expectans expectavi . . .		Et statuit . . .			Et immisit . . .
THEMATIC MATERIAL					Fugue 2 subject	Fugue 1 subject		Fugue 1 and 2 subjects

four-voice instrumental fugue (Fugue 1), whose subject's angularity contrasts with a countersubject moving in flowing stepwise motion. The subject entries follow the expected pattern, with the first statement on C in the oboe followed by a slightly extended "real" answer on G in the flute that preserves the same intervallic pattern.

After two more subject entries on C and G, and a short episode in the flutes based on the countersubject, Stravinsky introduces the chorus with a second four-voice fugue (Fugue 2). This is accompanied by Fugue 1's subject in the cellos and basses, with material derived from Fugue 1's countersubject appearing in the winds. Stravinsky then writes short stretto passages, featuring closely overlapped entries of the Fugue 2 subject, first for unaccompanied chorus, and then just for the instruments based on the Fugue 1 subject. After a dramatic general pause, Stravinsky has all the forces sound together in a developmental episode that combines variants of the two main subjects.

In contrast to the two outer movements, which feature interactions between modal and octatonic collections, the second movement of the *Symphony of Psalms* alludes to tonality. The instrumental fugue implies C minor, while the choral fugue suggests E♭ minor. As noted earlier, in both fugues the subject entries are arranged in the traditional tonic and dominant versions, and there are echoes of an augmented sixth preparing the dominant in measure 5 with the A♭ and F♯ implying a resolution to G.

In general, however, little in the voice-leading or the very free dissonance treatment emphasizes triads or tonal harmonic functions. More significant are the motivic relationships, starting with the opening subject, which can be heard as a series of statements of the (0134) pitch-class set with its two interlocked minor thirds (B–D; C–E♭) in measures 1–3 and (A–C; B♭–D♭) in measure 4. Both the minor third and (0134) are important throughout the work; they figure prominently, for example, in the ostinato figure in the first movement (E–G; F–A♭), and in the relationship between C and E♭ in the two fugue subjects in the second movement.

9

MAURICE RAVEL (1875–1937)

Concerto in G for Piano and Orchestra: Movement 1

Piano concerto, 1931

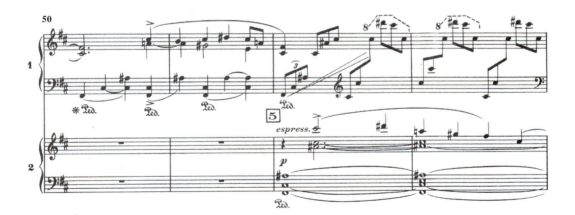

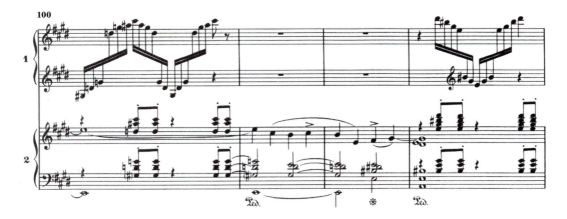

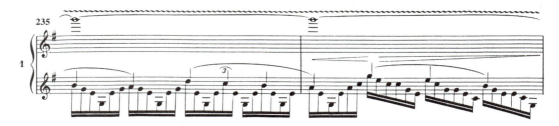

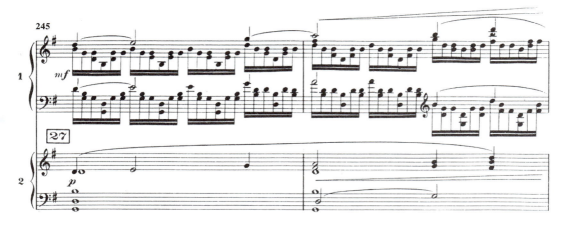

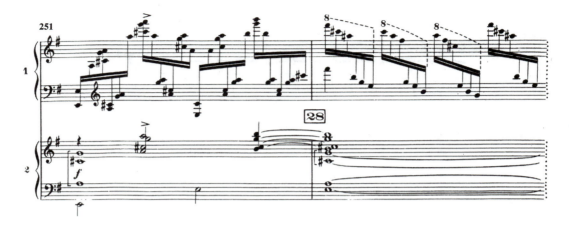

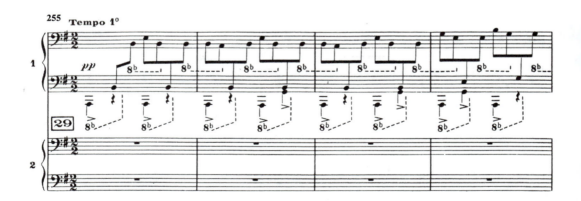

271

275

279

One of Ravel's last works, the Concerto in G was dedicated to the French pianist Marguerite Long, who gave the premiere in 1932. It illustrates the heterogeneous mix of materials available to composers in Paris between the world wars, including Neoclassical forms and genres, jazz and other popular styles, and the sounds of the Machine Age. Some passages in the recapitulation evoke gamelan music, while others in the development section recall the dissonant syncopated chords of Stravinsky's *Rite of Spring* (see Anthology 6).

In keeping with the Classical connotations of the genre, Ravel's Concerto calls for a small orchestra with eight first and eight second violins, six violas and six cellos, and four basses. Yet he expands the wind section to include piccolo, flute, oboe, English horn, and two each of clarinets, bassoons, horns, trumpets, and trombones. Passages in the winds evoke jazz techniques of flutter tongue, glissandi, and blue notes. Throughout the work he uses contrasts in texture, rhythm, timbre, and dynamics, more than melodic or harmonic development, to differentiate the appearances of the main themes and to build a sense of climax.

Ravel uses Classical forms in all three movements of the concerto, with the opening sonata form, a slow **ABA** middle movement, and a closing rondo. Yet there is nothing schematic about the first-movement form. Some interpret it as a sonata form without development, while others identify a development section. The latter is the reading we will follow here:

FORM	Exposition				Development	Recapitulation				Coda
MEASURES	1–106				107–171	172–254				255–323
			Second Group					Second Group		
THEME	FT	Trans.	ST	CT		FT	Trans.	ST	CT	
FIRST MEASURE	1	37	44	75		172	184	191	230	
KEY (I = G)	I		vii	VI		I		ii	I	I

Ravel employs unorthodox means to create a sense of tonal centers, frequently using ostinatos and pedals rather than functional progressions. At the beginning, for example, a whiplash sets in motion a bright tune in G major that is accompanied in the piano by a polytonal combination of a G-major triad and an F♯-major triad with an added sixth. The first unambiguous arrival on a G-major triad comes in measure 25, prepared by a nine-measure passage of parallel triads and dramatic piano glissandi from **d′** to **d″″** in place of a clear dominant.

Ravel preferred sudden shifts in harmony to gradual modulations, as shown by the abrupt jump to B minor at the start of the transition (Trans.) in measure 37. While the pentatonic first theme (FT) has often been heard as having a "Spanish" character (recalling Ravel's Basque heritage on his mother's side), the second group takes us to the world of blues and jazz. The languorous second theme (ST) is introduced by the piano, with short interpolations like improvisatory solo jazz breaks in the clarinet and muted trumpet. The prominent A♯/A♮ blue note results from the polymodal combination of an accompaniment in F♯ major and a melody in F♯ Phrygian. The lush closing theme (CT) in E major first appears in the piano and is then taken over by the orchestra. Both the second and the closing themes are in two parts and feature the added sevenths and motion to the subdominant characteristic of the blues.

To the generally relaxed character of the second group Ravel adds occasional syncopated passages (mm. 78–79), as if to suggest that the energetic character of the first theme is barely being held in check. And indeed it bursts out again in the brief development section, which reworks the first and second themes in a toccata-like style—featured in several of his late works—that Ravel identified as having mechanistic, Machine Art connotations.

The recapitulation goes through the same sequence of materials as the exposition, but in considerably altered form, particularly in the second group, which reappears with mysterious and dreamlike orchestral effects featuring the harp and the winds. Rather than giving the pianist a traditional solo cadenza—apart from the short scalar passage that functions as a retransition (m. 171)—Ravel makes a cadenza out of the first section of the closing theme, now back in the tonic and heavily ornamented with trills, while the left hand provides a virtuosic flowing accompaniment. After a climactic return of the closing theme, Ravel returns to his mechanistic style in the toccata-like coda to conclude the work.

10

ARNOLD SCHOENBERG (1874–1951)

Piano Piece, Op. 33a
Piano piece, 1929

Used by permission of Belmont Music Publishers.

Schoenberg's Op. 33 consists of two short twelve-tone pieces, Op. 33a (1929) and Op. 33b (1931), that were premiered in 1931 by the pianist Elsa Kraus. In keeping with Schoenberg's goal of producing "comprehensibility" through the logic of the musical development, Op. 33a combines the twelve-tone method with traditional compositional techniques. Op. 33a features a sonata form, including two contrasting themes—the second with a more lyrical character, a developmental central section, and a recapitulation that brings back the two themes from the exposition in a compressed form. Along with elements of the row structure discussed below, Schoenberg defines the form through traditional means, using contrasts in texture, rhythm, and tempo.

FORM	Exposition			Development		Recapitulation			Coda
MEASURES	1–23			23–32		32–36			37–40
THEME	FT	Trans.	ST			FT	Trans.	ST	
FIRST MEASURE	1	10	14			32	34	35	
ROW STRUCTURE	P^0/I^5			P^2/I^7	P^7/I^0	P^0/I^5			
	R^0/RI^5				R^7/RI^0	R^0/RI^5			

Following present-day practice, we have labeled the row forms using integer notation counting the number of half steps up from the starting pitch. Thus P^0 refers to the row beginning on B♭, P^2 transposes it up two half steps to C, and P^7 is the transposition up seven half steps to F. I^0 is the inversion of the row starting on B♭, and I^5 is the inversion transposed up five half steps to E♭. Retrogrades are identified by the pitch they end on; the retrograde of the prime form of the row is R^0, while the retrograde of the I^5 inversion is RI^5.

Through an analogy to the role of modulation in tonal music, Schoenberg used transpositions of the row followed by a return to the original form to create a sense of closure. And while B♭ is not established as a tonic around which the other pitches are hierarchically arrayed as in tonal music, it is emphasized throughout to define points of arrival, most strongly with the recapitulation of the opening material in measure 32. Unlike in some of his larger sonata-form movements, Schoenberg does not use transpositions of the row to differentiate the first theme from the second. His manuscript for the piece (see Fig. 7.1 in *Music in the Twentieth and Twenty-First Centuries*) suggests that he began with the intention of basing the entire work on the two row forms P^0/I^5, along with their retrogrades R^0/RI^5, deciding to introduce transpositions only as he began composing the development section. The transpositions he chooses (P^0, P^2, P^7; starting on B♭–C–F) suggest I, II, V in a tonal context. These three pitches also are included in the opening trichord of the row, thus linking the overall form of the piece to the structure of the row itself.

In much of Op. 33a Schoenberg uses two forms of the row simultaneously (a practice he applied to most of his twelve-tone works). Thus after chordal statements of P^0 in measure 1 and RI^5 in measure 2, in measures 3–5 the right hand presents RI^5 while the left hand provides R^0. His combining of these two forms of the row without doubling pitches—and thus without inadvertently arousing tonal expectations—depends on the property now called hexachordal combinatoriality. A row is combinatorial if there is at least one transformation, besides the retrograde, where the first half, or hexachord, shares no pitches with the first hexachord of the original row. And if a row is combinatorial, it follows that its transformations are as well, because they share the same intervallic patterns. Thus in Op. 33a just as P^0 and I^5 are combinatorial, so too are the other pairs of row forms Schoenberg employs, P^2/I^7 and P^7/I^0.

Besides guaranteeing the regular circulation of all twelve pitch classes, hexachordal combinatoriality integrates harmony and melody, resulting in what Schoenberg called "the unity of musical space." For example, the four-note harmonies that are produced by combining the first two pitches of P^0 and I^5 (B♭–F; E♭–A♭), as well as those produced by combining the last two pitches of the two rows (D–E; B–A), can both be abstracted to the same pitch-class set, which can be labeled as (0257) and represented as the pitches C–D–F–G. These four-note harmonies, or tetrachords (A♭–B♭–E♭–F and A–B–D–E), can be arranged into stacks of perfect fourths or fifths (for example, D–A–E–B) audibly recalling the stacked fourths of the opening trichord of the row. Thus because Schoenberg frequently presents the two combinatorial row forms P^0 and I^5 together throughout the piece, we often hear melodies and harmonies emphasizing perfect fourths and fifths, resulting in a unified sound world (see, for example, mm. 3, 5, 12, 14, and 23).

Using the row as a source of motives, Schoenberg sometimes adopted a flexible approach to ordering and repeating pitches. This, along with the occasional incomplete row (as in m. 20, where the final two pitches of R^0 and RI^5 are lacking; or m. 28, where we hear only the first hexachords of P^2/I^7 and P^7/I^0), can complicate the analysis, but results in a richer musical experience. While in other works some deviations from the row are actually misprints, Schoenberg was at times willing to go against the row structure for motivic reasons, resulting in what might appear to be occasional "wrong notes." For example, in the right hand in measure 22 Schoenberg writes A♮ instead of A♭ (which allows him to have another perfect fifth with the following D); and on the last beat of measure 35 he indicates B♮ instead of B♭ (which makes a connection with the important C–B dyad from P^0).

11

ANTON WEBERN (1883–1945)

Symphony, Op. 21: Movement 2, Variations
Symphony, 1928

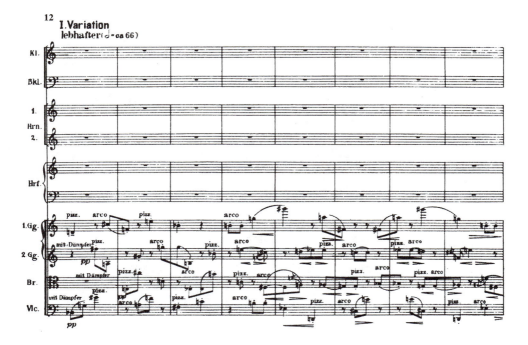

Webern composed his Symphony, Op. 21 in Vienna in 1927–28; the League of Composers premiered the work in New York the following year. Written for a chamber orchestra—the string parts can also be played by a quartet—the Symphony illustrates the complex structures and careful control of rhythm, dynamics, and other musical parameters that made Webern's music so interesting to composers after World War II. At the same time, its traditional genre, forms, and compositional techniques reflect Webern's affirmation of the twelve-tone method as an outgrowth of the past.

We can hear both traditional and forward-looking elements in Webern's approach to the theme-and-variations form in the Symphony's second movement: a theme, seven variations, and a coda. While he preserves the 11-measure length of the theme in each of the variations, he focuses less on its melodic and harmonic features than on its various perfect and imperfect symmetries—an emphasis that is evident in the movement's many palindromes. Variation III, for example, contains several small palindromes (see the clarinet in mm. 35–36 and 36–37), and the variation as a whole is also palindromic, with measure 39 as the midpoint. But just as important is Webern's practice of disrupting such symmetries so that the music remains developmental and propulsive. As with his penchant for embedding twelve-tone rows deeply in the music's structure rather than making them explicit on the surface, his goal was to create musical analogs to the mystical unity he believed to underlie the richness and diversity of the natural world.

Webern establishes the idea of disrupted symmetries in the structure of the theme (mm. 1–11). The clarinet presents a statement of P^0: F–Ab–G–F#–Bb–A–Eb–E–C–C#–D–B. The 48 row forms are provided in the 12-by-12 matrix on the following page. The row itself has a kind of mirror structure, with the second hexachord consisting of a retrograde of the first transposed up a tritone. An accompaniment in the harp and horns uses the retrograde (R^0). Had Webern presented this row in the same rhythm as the clarinet, the result would have been a mirrored series of tritones, such as we hear at the beginning (F–B), middle (A–Eb; A–Eb), and end (B–F) of the theme. By varying the rhythmic presentation he creates a diverse pattern of single notes, dyads, and trichords, along with a rich range of sonorities, including perfect fourths in measures 3 and 9, an interval that is not found in the basic row. And yet, while the specific pitches are different in the two halves, the theme is palindromic not only in the tone-color melody produced by the various combinations of instruments, but also in the rhythm, textural density, dynamics, and articulation.

Webern explores similar ideas in the movement's many mirror canons which include canon in inversion (Variation V), double canon in inversion with two themes (Variations I, II, VI, and VII), and retrograde canon with the second voice answering in reverse (Variation III). In some sections the canonic structures are relatively clear to see in the score, as in Variation I, starting with the upbeat to measure 12, with violin 1 (P^7) answered in inversion by the cello (I^5), and violin 2 (R^7) answered in inversion by the viola (RI^5). But in most cases Webern deliberately obscures the imitative relationships by breaking up the canonic voices among different instruments. In Variation II, for example, P^2 moves from G–Bb in the cello (m. 23) to A–G# in the bass clarinet and harp (m. 24). This is answered by I^{10} starting with Eb–C in the clarinet (mm. 23–24) and continuing with C#–D in the harp and bass clarinet (m. 24). Even more obscure, the French horn melody in Variation II can also be understood as a canon in inversion, with mirroring statements of I^0 (F–D–Eb, etc.) and P^{11} (E–G–Gb, etc.) presented by alternating notes of the single line. In keeping with the idea of disrupted symmetries, the harp, bass clarinet, and clarinet are palindromic in this variation, reaching the midpoint in measures 28–29, but the horn part moves constantly forward.

Webern makes the movement a large-scale palindrome by mirroring the pattern of expressive characters over the course of the work, with the feeling of the serene opening theme returning at the midpoint in Variation IV (which uses row forms R^2, P^6, RI^1, I^5) and in the coda at the end. He also associates the energetic pointillism of Variations I and VII; the ironic Neoclassical marches of Variations II and VI; and the anxiously obsessive repetitions of Variations III

Inversions (read down)

	I^0	I^3	I^2	I^1	I^5	I^4	I^{10}	I^{11}	I^7	I^8	I^9	I^6	
P^0	F	Ab	G	F#	Bb	A	Eb	E	C	C#	D	B	R^0
P^9	D	F	E	Eb	G	F#	C	C#	A	Bb	B	Ab	R^9
P^{10}	Eb	F#	F	E	Ab	G	C#	D	Bb	B	C	A	R^{10}
P^{11}	E	G	F#	F	A	Ab	D	Eb	B	C	C#	Bb	R^{11}
P^7	C	Eb	D	C#	F	E	Bb	B	G	Ab	A	F#	R^7
P^8	C#	E	Eb	D	F#	F	B	C	Ab	A	Bb	G	R^8
P^2	G	Bb	A	Ab	C	B	F	F#	D	Eb	E	C#	R^2
P^1	F#	A	Ab	G	B	Bb	E	F	C#	D	Eb	C	R^1
P^5	Bb	C#	C	B	Eb	D	Ab	A	F	F#	G	E	R^5
P^4	A	C	B	Bb	D	C#	G	Ab	E	F	F#	Eb	R^4
P^3	Ab	B	Bb	A	C#	C	F#	G	Eb	E	F	D	R^3
P^6	B	D	C#	C	E	Eb	A	Bb	F#	G	Ab	F	R^6
	RI^0	RI^3	RI^2	RI^1	RI^5	RI^4	RI^{10}	RI^{11}	RI^7	RI^8	RI^9	RI^6	

Prime forms (read left to right)

Retrogrades (read right to left)

Retrograde inversions (read up)

The 48 versions of the row of a twelve-tone piece (12 transpositions P^0–P^{11}; 12 inversions I^0–I^{11}; 12 retrogrades R^0–R^{11}; 12 retrograde inversions RI^0–RI^{11}) can be represented efficiently in the 12-by-12 matrix or "magic square." This matrix for Op. 21 is constructed by writing the prime form of the row (P^0) along the top row and the inversion of the row (I^0) down the left side. The transpositions of the prime form can then be filled in moving down the table following the order of the inversion. The labels on the sides show where the various row forms can be found; this square is labeled in reference to F=0, F#=1, G=2, Ab=3, etc. Thus P^0 is the prime form starting on F; I^1 is the inversion starting on F#; R^2 is the retrograde of the prime form that starts on G; and RI^3 is the retrograde of the inversion that starts on Ab. Due to the symmetries of this particular row, some forms of the row duplicate others exactly. Thus P^0=R^6 and R^0=P^6.

and V (I^3, RI^3, P^6, R^6), with each pair of associated variations using the same row forms. But at the same time he reinforces a sense of forward movement by giving each variation a different instrumentation, with the full ensemble appearing only in Variations IV and VII.

BÉLA BARTÓK (1881–1945)

Music for Strings, Percussion, and Celesta: Movement 1

Chamber orchestra piece, 1936

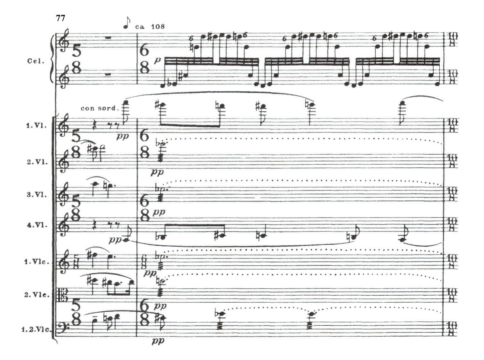

Bartók composed the *Music for Strings, Percussion, and Celesta* on commission from the Basel Chamber Orchestra and its conductor, Paul Sacher, who premiered it in 1937. Bartók specified in the score that the strings were to be divided into two groups, with the percussion positioned between them. The spatial separation clarifies the textural complexities of the first movement and permits dramatic antiphonal effects later in the work.

	Double bass I	Double bass II	
Cello I	Timpani	Bass Drum	Cello II
Viola I	Side Drums	Cymbals	Viola II
Violin II	Celesta	Xylophone	Violin IV
Violin I	Piano	Harp	Violin III

The forms of the first three movements demonstrate Bartók's Neoclassical leanings: I is a fugue, II a sonata form, and III a version of his "bridge form" (in this case, **ABCBA**), which he also labeled a rondo. We can also hear the influence of Hungarian and other folk musics, particularly in the series of short dancelike sections in the final movement. The rhythmic structure of the first movement's fugue subject alludes to the additive rhythms of Bulgarian music, built up from two- and three-beat rhythmic cells.

In his analytical note in the score, Bartók identified the first movement of the *Music for Strings, Percussion, and Celesta* as being "in A," but as is clear from the scarcity of triads or functional harmonic progressions, his interest here is in developing new ways of creating tonal centricity. He concludes the coda with a two-measure passage (mm. 86–88) that uses symmetrical structures to emphasize a pitch within a chromatically saturated context. The first and second violins present the second phrase of the fugue subject in both its original and inverted forms, beginning on A, expanding out above and below to E♭ and E♭, then contracting back to the starting point. The symmetrical lines, which together provide a complete chromatic collection, thus establish A as the focal point, or inversional center. The tonal centers for the four movements (A–C–F♯–A) are likewise arrayed symmetrically a minor third above and below the focal point of A.

This passage in the coda also encapsulates the overall form of the movement, described by Bartók as a fugue based on a series of subject entries that start on A and then proceed through a sequence a fifth above and a fifth below, continuing until they reach the most distant point of E♭/D♯ (see the following table). Bartók then reverses the process, using the inversion of the subject to move back through the cycle of fifths to A. The chromatic unfolding of the subject (mm. 1–4) presents all the pitches between a and e′, while the "real" answer (mm. 5–8) fills in the rest of the chromatic scale between e′ and b′. The subject entries similarly move through all twelve pitch classes.

FORM	Exposition					Episode	Stretto					Episode		Episode
MEASURE	1	4	8	12	16	21	26	27	33	34	35	37	44	46
		E	B				F♯			C♯	G♯			
ENTRY PITCH	A												E♭	
		D		G				C	F		B♭			

FORM	Stretto										Coda
MEASURE	56	58	61	64	65	68	69	72	73	77	82
		(B♭)	(F)	C		G		D			
ENTRY PITCH	E♭									A	
		A♭			F♯		B		E		

But this neat description is inadequate to the intriguing complexity of the movement, just as the marking Andante tranquillo does not prepare us for the intensity and strangeness of later passages. What starts as a clear and systematic process in the exposition, with the first five entries of the subject, begins to break down as lines pile up into a thick web, while the accompanying voices and episode material become freer and more developmental. The subsequent subject entries are increasingly obscured by octave displacements, close stretti (mm. 26–36), and the fragmentation of the subject (the B♭ and G♯ entries in measure 35, for example, are represented only by the second phrase), so much so that scholars dispute their precise location.

The contrapuntal texture also gives way in the second episode (mm. 37ff.) as the individual voices lose their independence and begin to move together, culminating in the unison E♭s of measure 56. This shift away from the individual lines is intensified by the surprising entrance of the percussion, with the low rumble of the timpani (mm. 34–38, 53–56), the bright white noise of the cymbal (mm. 51–52), and the loud blow of the bass drum with the climactic E♭s.

The clarity of the structure is further obscured as the formal processes reverse, with the inverted subject entries represented by only short fragments (E♭ in m. 56 and A♭ in m. 58) or by a single note (the B♭ and F in mm. 58 and 61); the D♭ entry is missing entirely. When we return to the starting point on A, we hear the subject in both original and inverted forms, but Bartók introduces the celesta to absorb them into his characteristic mysterious "night music" sound world, to which he will return in the third movement. The effect is less of closure than an opening out toward the new horizons the theme will explore in the following movements.

Billy the Kid Suite, "Street in a Frontier Town" (excerpt)

Ballet, 1938

With its Western frontier setting and prominent use of American folk songs, *Billy the Kid* was central to Copland's creation of a musical Americana. From its premiere in 1938 in a version for two pianos, with the orchestral version following in 1939, the ballet has been one of Copland's most successful works. It is also frequently performed in the concert suite version excerpted here, also from 1939, which preserves about two-thirds of the original 30-minute ballet.

The American dancer and actor Eugene Loring created the scenario, about the life of the legendary frontier outlaw. The work begins and ends "on the open prairie" (Lento maestoso). The empty stage is gradually filled by a somber westward procession of "pioneers, men, women, Mexicans and Indians," represented with stylized modern dance choreography. The 12-year-old Billy first appears with his mother as a bystander in the scene called "Street in a Frontier Town" (Moderato). The stage directions read: "Familiar figures amble by. Cowboys saunter into town, some on horseback, others with their lassoes. Some Mexican women do a jarabe which is interrupted by a fight between two drunks." The scene starts lightheartedly, but when his mother is accidentally killed in the brawl, Billy begins his life as an outlaw by pulling out a knife and stabbing those responsible to death.

Copland started work on *Billy the Kid* during a visit to Paris, and the music shows the influence of his earlier years there, including Milhaud's polytonality and polyrhythm, and Stravinsky's techniques of developing folk materials through rhythmic transformation, repetition, and the layering of other elements. But the ballet also reflects Copland's commitment to adapting these techniques in a way that was accessible to a broad public. He emphasizes diatonic melodies and harmonies, and presents the musical ideas with a clarity that is easy for listeners to follow.

"Street in a Frontier Town" includes several cowboy songs that Copland freely adapted from published collections. The first tune is "Great Granddad," in A♭ major, to be played nonchalantly on a tin whistle by one of the cowboys, or by the piccolo in the concert version (mm. 1–8). Copland develops this simple melody, with its limited range and pitch content, by varying the rhythm, texture, register, dynamics, and timbre. He accompanies the first statement with a dominant pedal on E♭. After a transitional passage on the tonic, based on three-note motives from the tune (mm. 9–15), "Great Granddad" returns in octaves in the piccolo and clarinet, partly doubled by pizzicato violins that bring out other three-note motives in the tune.

To capture the bustling action of the street, Copland employs polytonality, counterpointing the two phrases of "Great Granddad" (mm. 16–19 and 24–27) in A♭ major with another tune based on "Whoopee Ti Yi Yo, Git Along Little Dogies," presented in F major (mm. 20–23 and 28–31). He playfully emphasizes the resulting clash between A♮ and A♭ when the cowboys apparently try to join together on "Whoopee Ti Yi Yo," without quite managing to get it right (mm. 32–39).

The grace-note figure at the end of the tune, which imitates the whoops and yodeling vocal effects made famous by "singing cowboys" like Tex Ritter, is transformed into a syncopated ostinato figure (mm. 40–56). This accompanies another statement of "Great Granddad," now in C major, doubled in sixths over an F pedal. Copland further enriches the texture by adding a syncopated countermelody in the brass (mm. 51–56).

As the scene gets more boisterous in measures 57–74, Copland reworks the two duple-meter tunes from measures 16–31 in off-kilter polyrhythmic opposition with a triadic waltzlike accompaniment, grouped in patterns of 3+3+2. In keeping with his ideal of "imposed simplicity," Copland combines the complicated rhythm and texture of this passage with a more straightforward D♭ tonality, with a clear tonic and dominant seventh alternation and no trace of the previous polytonal clashes.

Copland also varies the melody in the two statements of "Whoopee Ti Yi Yo" (mm. 61–65 and 70–74), as if the tune were trying to adapt to the new rhythm and mix of people on the street. This cultural intermingling becomes even more complex as the tune is further transformed in measures 75–84 to anticipate the melodic and rhythmic character of the driving $\frac{5}{8}$ jarabe dance that follows this excerpt to conclude the scene. But before that happens, the activity momentarily winds down so that everyone can catch their breaths and wait for more excitement to come along.

Africa, Part 2: *Land of Romance*

Symphonic poem, 1935

William Grant Still prepared several versions of his symphonic poem *Africa*, including an orchestral score premiered by the Rochester Philharmonic in 1930 and an arrangement of the third part for Paul Whiteman's jazz orchestra in 1933. Due to a dispute with a publisher, his revised score from 1935 was not published or recorded until more than 70 years later. This piano arrangement, also from 1935, is attributed to Still's second wife, Verna Avery.

Still described the work's three parts, *Land of Peace*, *Land of Romance*, and *Land of Superstition*, as representing an idealized Africa based on folklore and legend reimagined from an African-American perspective. He does not incorporate actual African music, but rather elements of the blues and jazz that had been given "African" connotations by pieces such as Darius Milhaud's *The Creation of the World* (1923) and Duke Ellington's works like the *Black and Tan Fantasy* (1927). *Land of Romance* features pervasive melodic blue notes, harmonies based on the minor/major seventh chord (m/M7), and textures suggesting a jazz rhythm section, with a syncopated melody over a steady accompaniment.

Still combines these elements with sinuous chromatic melodies and lush string scoring that evoke French Exoticist works like Maurice Ravel's *Schéhérazade* (1903). He builds on Claude Debussy's techniques of using chains of parallel triads and seventh chords. Passages of *Land of Romance* more directly recall Debussy's *Prelude to "The Afternoon of a Faun"* (1894), particularly in measures 73–75 and 86–95, which, like Debussy's work, allude to the "Tristan" chord from the Prelude to Wagner's *Tristan und Isolde*, thus linking Still's symphonic poem to other programmatic orchestral pieces exploring romantic desire.

TEMPO	Lento		Più mosso				Risoluto		Come primo	
FORM	**A**		**B**			**C**	**D**		**B′**	**A′**
MEASURES	1–34		35–65			66–79	80–107		108–121	122–139
FIRST MEASURE	1	17	35	46	56	66	80	95	108	122
THEME	**a**	**a′**	**b**	**b′**	transition	**c**	**d**	transition	**b″**	**a′**
HARMONY	G$^{m/M7}$		B♭$^{m/M7}$	F$^{m/M7}$	A$^{m/M7}$	E♭$^{m/M7}$	B♭$^{m/M7}$		G$^{m/M7}$	

Still described *Land of Romance* as mingling elements of romance, mystery, and sorrow. The six sections imply a narrative of a romantic encounter, starting in section **A** with a slow, solitary blues melody played by the bassoon over an open-fifth tonic pedal in the low strings (mm. 1–16). Arpeggiated piano chords provide both an accompaniment and a countermelody that introduces an important rising-and-falling motive (m. 2: F–G–D; m. 4: G–A–D). The piano arrangement omits a contrapuntal line in three flutes (mm. 7–11), as well as the jazzlike melodic interpolations, or fills, in the harp that answer the first two phrases of the bassoon melody (mm. 3–5).

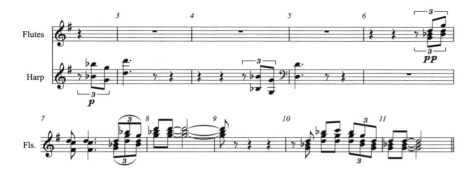

Still's talent as an arranger can be heard in his reworking of the opening melody in the second half of **A** (mm. 17–34), now with rich chromatic harmonies featuring minor/major seventh and ninth chords above a more active bass line.

Moving to B♭ minor/major, the faster (Più mosso) **B** section is more light-hearted, as though the protagonist has found a partner. Still introduces a new melody, based on the rising-and-falling motive, which we also hear in two versions. The dancelike first version features an ostinato rhythm in the accompaniment (mm. 35–45); the second setting, which moves to F$^{m/M7}$, is more tentative and harmonically unsettled (mm. 46–55). A transitional passage centered on A$^{m/M7}$ (mm. 56–65) introduces fragments of a yearning ascending melody that becomes the basis of the impassioned **C** section.

The exuberant and resolute (Risoluto) **D** section develops material from the opening of the **A** section, enlivened by a large-scale two-against-three hemiola as the duple melody and accompaniment interact with the prevailing triple meter (mm. 80–95). The melody integrates the chordal texture of the piano accompaniment from the **A** section with a descending chromatic line that alludes to the beginning of the blues melody in measure 1 (F♯–F–E♭–D). A violin countermelody (mm. 80–90, not included in the piano score) recalls the rising-and-falling motive.

Still develops the descending chromatic line as chains of parallel triads, seventh chords, and minor/major sevenths. In measures 104–107 he solidifies the connection between the descending parallel chords and the opening gesture of the blues melody by harmonizing the notes F♯–F–E♭–D with minor/major sevenths, a half-diminished seventh, and a V$^4_3$ to prepare the return to the original tonic and tempo.

Still's **B** section, reworked to feature two intertwining voices scored for winds, suggests a happy ending to the romance. Yet the return of the melancholy second part of the **A** section to conclude *Land of Romance* leaves the final outcome uncertain.

15

BENJAMIN BRITTEN (1913–1976)

War Requiem, Op. 66, Requiem aeternam
Choral work, 1961

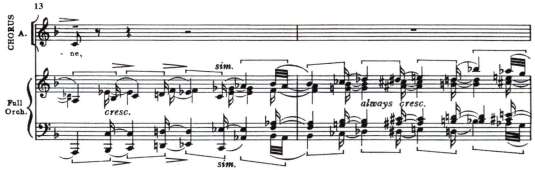

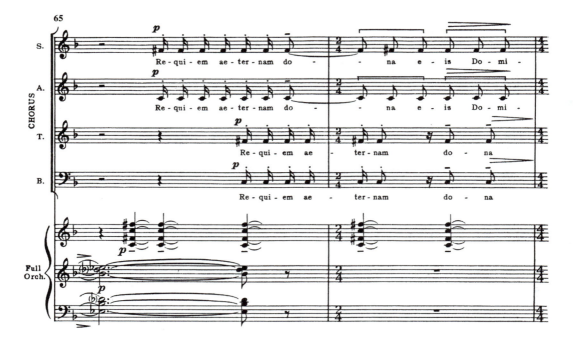

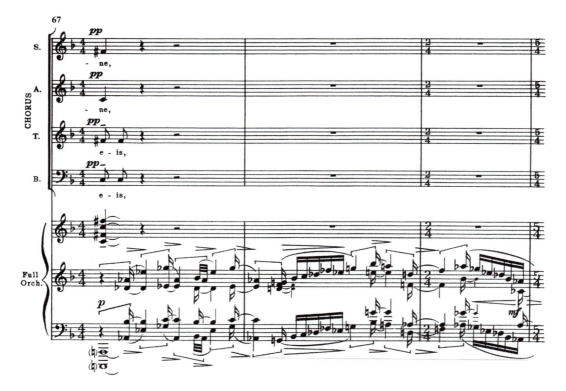

CHORUS

Requiem aeternam dona eis Domine;	*Eternal rest grant unto them, O Lord;*
et lux perpetua luceat eis.	*And let perpetual light shine upon them.*

BOYS

Te decet hymnus, Deus in Sion;	*To you we owe our hymn of praise, O God, in Sion;*
et tibi reddetur votum in Jerusalem;	*To you must vows be fulfilled in Jerusalem;*
exaudi orationem meam,	*Hear my prayer,*
ad te omnis caro veniet.	*To you all flesh must come.*

CHORUS

Requiem aeternam dona eis Domine;	*Eternal rest grant unto them, O Lord;*
et lux perpetua luceat eis.	*And let perpetual light shine upon them.*

TENOR

What passing-bells for these who die as cattle?
   Only the monstrous anger of the guns.
   Only the stuttering rifles' rapid rattle
Can patter out their hasty orisons.
No mockeries for them from prayers or bells,
   Nor any voice of mourning save the choirs,—
The shrill, demented choirs of wailing shells;
   And bugles calling for them from sad shires.
What candles may be held to speed them all?
   Not in the hands of boys, but in their eyes
Shall shine the holy glimmers of good-byes.
   The pallor of girls' brows shall be their pall;
Their flowers the tenderness of silent minds,
And each slow dusk a drawing-down of blinds.

CHORUS

Kyrie eleison	*Lord have mercy.*
Christe eleison	*Christ have mercy.*
Kyrie eleison	*Lord have mercy.*

Composed for the dedication of the new Coventry Cathedral, the *War Requiem* serves as both a memorial to the fallen in World War II and a denunciation of war. Britten brings together starkly contrasting materials, starting with the sacred Latin texts of the Requiem Mass for the Dead and nine poems in English by Wilfred Owen about his experiences in World War I.

The first of six movements, the Requiem aeternam corresponds to the Introit and Kyrie of the Mass. Interpolated among these calls for peace, rest, and mercy, Owen's sonnet "Anthem for Doomed Youth" is a bitter dismissal of the comforts offered by religious rituals in the face of the worldly realities of war. While the tenor soloist is accompanied by a 12-piece chamber orchestra, the Latin Mass texts are presented by the choir, accompanied by the orchestra, and by a boys' choir placed in the distance and supported by a portable organ. The musical materials also are marked by strong contrasts, including tonal, atonal, and serial passages. Britten uses an F♯–C dyad to integrate the diverse materials throughout the Requiem aeternam, but it is crucial to the overall meaning of the movement that the dissonant tritone can provide only a fractured and uncertain stability.

The overall **ABA'** form of the movement follows the alternation between the Latin and English texts; the internal tripartite structure of the first two sections also mirrors this form, but the brief third section breaks free from it. The "slow and solemn" opening choral section (section **A**, mm. 1–76) is punctuated by low tolling bells on F♯ and C, answered by the chorus on the same pitches. The metric ambiguity produced by constantly shifting meters intensifies the static and otherworldly quality. Answering the increasingly fervent choral phrases is a severe passage in the orchestra reminiscent of the characteristic dotted rhythms of the Baroque French overture form. While initially suggesting D minor, the harmonies slowly dissolve into the octatonic collection (C♯–D–E–F–G–A♭–B♭–B).

FORM	A				B		A'
	a	**b**	**a'**	**c**	**b'**	**c'**	
MEASURES	1–28	29–61	61–76	77–124	125–160	161–165	166–176
VOCALISTS	Chorus	Boys	Chorus	Tenor	Tenor		Chorus
TEXT	Requiem aeternam . . .	Te decet hymnus . . .	Requiem aeternam . . .	What passing-bells . . .	Not in the hands of boys . . .		Kyrie eleison . . .

The entry of the boys' choir (section **b**, mm. 29–61), with their bright timbre, faster tempo, and diatonic materials, makes a sharp contrast. Alluding to aspects of the twelve-tone method, the two antiphonal groups sing four-measure phrases accompanied by tonally unrelated major and minor triads that move systematically through all the pitches of the chromatic scale. Each four-measure vocal melody uses 11 out of the 12 pitches, with the answering vocal line a strict I^6 inversion of the original phrase (mm. 33–36). The F♯–C dyad continues to operate in the background defining the beginning and end of each phrase. It gradually becomes more pervasive as the vocal phrases are compressed and finally coalesce on the tritone to prepare for a shortened return of the choral opening (section **a′**, mm. 61–76).

Section **B** (mm. 77–165) starts suddenly, pulling us from an eternal sphere down into the worldly trenches. The F♯–C dyad is taken over by the harp tremolo and reinterpreted as G♭–C—part of a dominant ninth in B♭ minor. In a tempo marked "very quick and agitated," the tenor spits out Owen's words as a sharp rebuke to the music we have just heard. Britten employs word-painting, including the lurching march rhythm in the bass, the dissonant high gestures in the winds for the wailing shells, the sound of trumpets, and the drums evoking the patter of the rifles. Just as literal is the modified repetition of the boys' music in response to the line "Not in the hands of boys." But Britten breaks up the neat, angelic ordering of the original sequence of triads, just as Owen recasts the depersonalized and ritualized response to death through a series of metaphors that capture personal pain and loss. The tenor's section ends with a brief return of the opening march material and the G♭–C harp tremolo, which prepares for a return to the static choral music.

The movement ends with a chorale-like setting of the Kyrie eleison (section **A′**, mm. 166–176). For the first time in the work, the chorus struggles to break free from the F♯–C tritone; the final Kyrie manages a resolution to F major through a half-step Phrygian cadence, as if to offer an answer to the call for mercy in the text. F major had been suggested in the boys' music and elsewhere in the movement, but the conclusion still sounds tentative and provisional, as if to demonstrate both the necessity and the difficulty of finding some sort of reconciliation amid the rubble of war.

16

DMITRI SHOSTAKOVICH (1906–1975)

String Quartet No. 8, Op. 110: Movement 3
String quartet, 1960

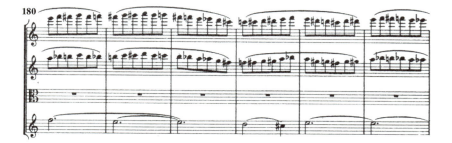

186

193

200

208

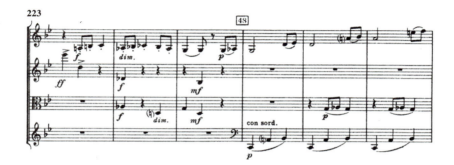

270

276

283

292

Shostakovich's String Quartet No. 8 grew out of his experience of seeing the bombed-out ruins of the German city of Dresden, but he also characterized the work as a kind of requiem for himself. Each of the five continuous movements features quotations from significant moments in his career—some hopeful, some teetering on the edge of despair—as he navigated the treacherous cultural politics of the Soviet Union. Shostakovich makes the autobiographical dimension audible by basing melodies on his musical signature: DSCH (D–E♭–C–B). Using thematic transformation, he places the motto in many situations and moods depending on the expressive and tonal context of each movement.

After the slow contrapuntal opening movement, the second and third movements evoke the playful, dancelike character of a scherzo, though in both cases the tone is brooding and sardonic. Like the second movement, the third-movement Allegretto implies what is sometimes called a double scherzo form, where the trio and scherzo sections are repeated (**ABABA**), though in both cases the expected scherzo return is truncated.

FORM	Scherzo			Trio			Scherzo			Trio		Coda
SECTION	Intro	A	B	A′	C	D	E	Intro	A	B	A′	C′	D′	F
FIRST MEASURE	1	17	67	102	117	140	153	190	207	226	245	260	270	283

The third movement begins with a sudden, dramatic statement of the DSCH motive, interrupting the maniacally driving rhythms of the preceding Allegro molto movement. After an introductory passage featuring the first violin's emphatic but uncertain chromatic melody, Shostakovich defines the **A** section (mm. 17–66) with a simple waltzlike accompaniment in G minor that has been compared to Saint-Saëns's *Danse macabre*. The DSCH motive then reappears, transformed into a repetitive dance tune in the character of a Russian folk melody. Playing against the sharply delineated metric profile of the tune, balanced phrase structure, and homophonic texture of both passages, Shostakovich employs sudden Stravinskyan metric displacements, such as those in measures 42–45. These shifts articulate the end of phrases but also evoke an image of drunken stumbling, intensified by the lurching rhythms of the **B** section (mm. 67–101).

The **A** section also illustrates the complexities of Shostakovich's harmonic language, which has proven resistant to analytical accounts despite its accessibility and effectiveness. As with this movement in G minor, many of his works have key signatures, but the key is established more by pedal tones and ostinati than by functional progressions. While it is often easy to identify the tonic triad, the pervasive chromaticism makes labeling other chords more challenging.

In the first movement, the pitches of Shostakovich's signature, D, E♭, C, and B, are consistent with the overall C-minor tonality. Here, in the scherzo's **A** section, in contrast, the B♮ in the motive, emphasized by the trill in the second violin, clashes with the B♭ of the accompanimental G-minor triads. Harmonizing the chromatic descending second phrase of the melody (mm. 25–28) is a chord built on the raised supertonic A♭ that has aspects of a Neapolitan sixth chord and an augmented sixth chord, but the overall effect is less a clearly defined harmony than a collection of neighbor notes to the tonic triad.

The **C** section of the trio begins in measure 117, with an unstable solo viola line recalling the introduction and answered by variants of the DSCH motive. The sudden appearance in measure 140 of the mockingly pompous march in B♭ (based on the transposed opening of Shostakovich's Cello Concerto No. 1, completed the previous year) defines section **D**. This passage from the concerto was itself a quotation from his film score *The Young Guard* (1948), for a section entitled *Procession to Execution*.

Instead of the expected return of the C section, there is a new section **E** (mm. 153–189), in which a haunting, high-register cello melody derived from the DSCH motive is accompanied by swirling chromatic motion in the violins. Repeating the sudden gesture that launched the movement, this section is stridently interrupted by the DSCH motive and a return of the scherzo. But now the mood is still more tentative and uncertain, with all the instruments muted and at a soft dynamic. As if unable to summon up the energy for a full return, the trio's **C′** (mm. 260–269) and **D′** (mm. 270–282) sections are considerably compressed. The movement finally disintegrates into a wandering and disconsolate single line that, with its *Dies Irae* quotation, sets the tone for the grim movement that follows.

17

PIERRE BOULEZ (B. 1925)

Le marteau sans maître, Movement 5: *Bel édifice et les pressentiments*, first version

Chamber song cycle, 1955

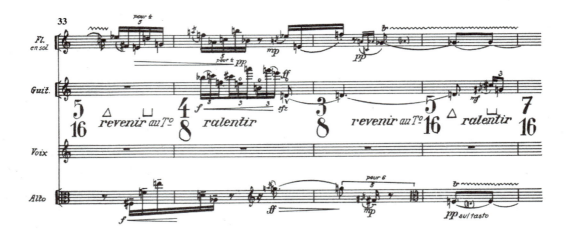

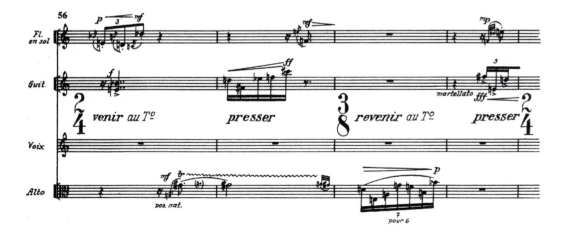

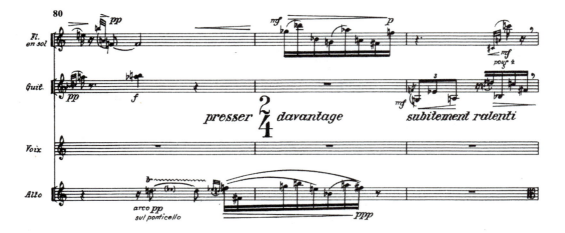

J'écoute marcher dans mes jambes	*I hear marching in my legs*
La mer morte vagues par-dessus tête	*The dead sea waves overhead*
Enfant la jetée-promenade sauvage	*Child the wild walk on the wharf*
Homme l'illusion imitée	*Man the imitated illusion*
Des yeux purs dans les bois	*Pure eyes in the woods*
Cherchent en pleurant la tête habitable.	*Seek weeping the habitable head.*

Boulez composed *Le marteau sans maître* (The Hammer without a Master) between 1953 and 1955, using three poems from a 1934 collection by the French Surrealist poet René Char. He structures its nine movements as three asymmetrical and intersecting cycles associated with each poem. In addition to the actual setting in movement 3, the cycle for "Furious Artisanry" (movements 1, 3, and 7) includes instrumental "before" and "after" movements. "Executioners of Solitude" (2, 4, 6, and 8), the largest cycle, has three "commentaries" framing the poem in movement 6. The cycle for "Beautiful Building and Premonitions" (5 and 9) is the only one in which the poem is set twice, with the ninth movement, labeled "Beautiful Building and Premonitions, Double," serving as both a variation on the fifth movement and a finale for the whole set.

In "Beautiful Building and Premonitions" the music follows the form of the text, with polyphonic instrumental sections in a lively tempo (which we will call sections I, III, and V) alternating with settings of the three paired lines in a slower tempo and primarily homophonic texture (sections II, IV, and VI).

FORM	I	II	III	IV	V	VI
MEASURES	1–14	15–29	30–62	63–88	89–109	110–117
TEXT		J'écoute marcher . . .		Enfant la jetée . . .		Des yeux purs . . .

Inspired by Char's deliberately elusive style, Boulez creates an amorphous, nonlinear sense of time, which he also attributed to the influence of Asian music. This static, atemporal quality can be heard in "Beautiful Building and Premonitions" at every level of the structure, including the irregular rhythms of the individual parts in each measure, the constantly changing meters and fluctuating tempi, and the many silences that disrupt any sense of pulse (see especially mm. 39–52).

Recalling Schoenberg's *Pierrot lunaire* (see Anthology 3), *Le marteau sans maître* features a contralto employing a range of vocal techniques from speaking to singing, including Sprechstimme in measures 19, 21, 62–63, and 117. Boulez uses a small mixed ensemble, though with six rather than the five instrumentalists that Schoenberg used: alto flute (which sounds a perfect fourth lower than written), viola, guitar (which sounds an octave lower than written), xylorimba (an instrument that combines the ranges of the xylophone and marimba and which sounds an octave higher than written), vibraphone, and percussion. Boulez has also suggested exotic connotations for the scintillating sound world of *Marteau*, writing that the xylorimba was intended to evoke the African balafon, the vibraphone referred to the Balinese gender (a xylophone-like instrument), and the guitar was a stand-in for the Japanese koto.

"Beautiful Building and Premonitions" uses only viola, voice, guitar, and flute. The piece exemplifies Boulez's elegant approach to orchestration, with subtle interactions between the instruments resulting from heterophonic textures where two or more instruments simultaneously unfold closely related melodies (see mm. 9–10 and 31–40). Often the musicians seem to finish each others' thoughts: note, for example, the c#″ passed from viola to flute in measure 7; the entrance of the voice on eb′ in measure 15, which emerges from the sustained flute trill; and the timbral link between the guitar and pizzicato viola in measures 105–108.

Inspired by the opening of the first movement of Webern's Symphony, Op. 21 (see Anthology 11), Boulez fixes each of the twelve tones in a specific register. For example, as illustrated in the chart below, the viola opens with a series of twelve pitches (mm. 1–4, first sixteenth note) that returns precisely in the same register, though in a different ordering, in the concluding measures of the voice (mm. 114–117). In other words, when we hear an E♮ in these two passages, it is the e′ above middle C; the lowest note is the F♮ below middle C, and so on.

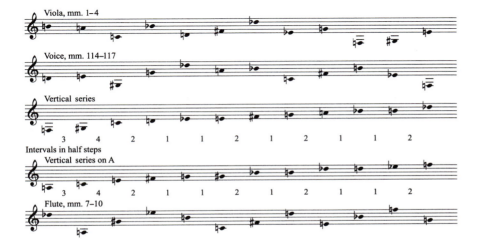

Boulez arranges the twelve pitches from lowest to highest, resulting in the pattern of intervals (measured in half steps) 3, 4, 2, 1, 1, 2, 1, 2, 1, 1, 2. This, in turn, enables him to generate other melodic lines by transposing this "vertical series," as the technique has been labeled, to other starting points. For example, as shown at the bottom of the chart, the pitches of the flute part in measures 7–10 (excluding the repeated final two pitches D and C♯ in m. 10) can be arranged into the same pattern of intervals from lowest to highest, transposed up a major third to start on the note A below middle C.

Fixing the pitches in specific registers also contributes to the static, nondirectional, floating quality of the music, as the focus turns away from a linear unfolding of rows to more generalized sound fields defined by the different types of intervals available in the various registers.

PAULINE OLIVEROS (B. 1932)

Traveling Companions

Indeterminate work for percussion and dancers, 1980

For percussion ensemble and dancers (minimum of 2 percussionists and 2 dancers)

Traveling Companions is intended for an outdoor space such as a public park. If outdoor space is impractical then indoor space such as a large gymnasium could be suitable. The length of the performance is indefinite.

The percussionists should be set up at the maximum distances from each other which still allows for hearing each other well. Dancers should be able to move through maximum distances in relation to hearing the percussionists and seeing the other dancers. Audience members should be able to come and go as they are attracted to the event. Audience members should also be able to observe at any distance from the performers they so choose.

INSTRUCTIONS

Each percussionist should have equal resources.

In the center of the chart, the word *equal* refers to everyone playing or dancing exactly the same thing in the same way at the same time, either during the agreed upon beginning or during moments that occur naturally during the course of the performance.

At the 8 points around the chart are 4 sets of opposites: less-more, slower-faster, simpler-complexer and softer-louder (smaller-larger for dancers). These opposites are contained in 4 attributes which players or dancers must perceive in order to participate in the piece:

1. Density which means the frequency or number of events occurring in relation to the tempo.

2. Tempo which means the rate of speed underlying the events.

3. Timbre which means the quality of the sound or sounds and the kind of movement or movements in use.

4. Volume which means the loudness or dynamics of events.

Baltimore, MD: Smith Publications, 1998. Reprinted with permission.

PROCEDURE

After an agreed upon or predetermined equal beginning, when any performer* perceives a difference in another performers playing or dancing in any of the 4 attributes, then one of the following choices may be made:

A. Change your playing or dancing so that all attributes are again equal to the other performer. (*Percussionists always refer to percussionists and dancers to dancers.)

B. Play or dance opposite to the perceived possibility, i.e. if someone is doing more, do less.

C. Choose any of the other possibilities, i.e. if someone is doing more, do slower, faster, simpler, complexer, softer (smaller) or louder (larger).

D. Play or dance in competition to the perceived possibility, i.e. if someone is doing *more*, then do more than that performer.

The chart shows all of the possible combinations of these choices. Each performer should attempt to cover all 8 possibilities during the course of the performance or a cycle of the performance, using *equal* (to one or all performers) as a resting point after each other choice.

July 7, 1980
Saugerties, New York

Oliveros has characterized ritualistic works like *Traveling Companions* (1980) as musical "software for people" that uses words and images to elicit actions that encourage attentiveness to, and engagement with, sound, our physical selves, the environment, and each other. As with works by John Cage, the goal of *Traveling Companions* is to break down the borders between art and life. In keeping with this ideal, Oliveros specifies a performance context that allows the audience to move freely among the performers as the work unfolds, preferably in a parklike outdoor space. In the analysis that follows, readers are encouraged to consider a range of possible realizations of the piece, including performances they might organize.

Traveling Companions illustrates the connections between ways of thinking and hearing associated with Indeterminacy, electronic music, texture music, and participatory "happenings." The score, which consists of two pages of

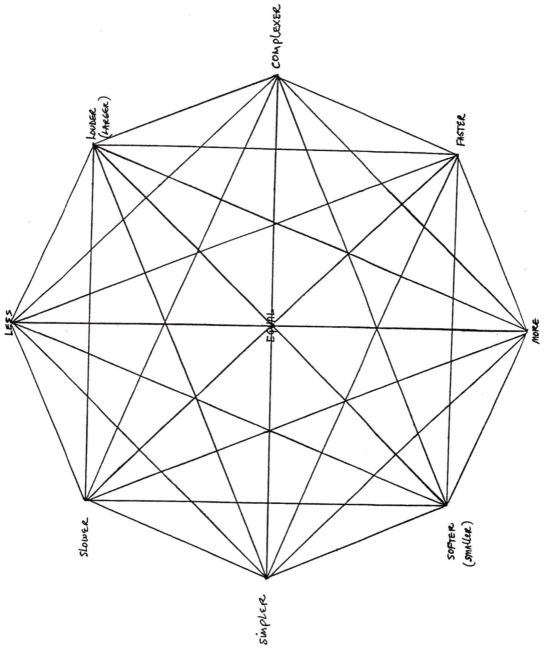

directions and a diagram, leaves a great many details indeterminate. It calls for two or more dancers, along with a percussion ensemble of two or more players, who are each to have the same collection of instruments. The percussionists and dancers interact with each other according to a set of eight possibilities and all their combinations, as indicated on the diagram: less-more, slower-faster, simpler-complexer, softer-louder (for the dancers, smaller-larger). Reflecting her background in electronic music, Oliveros specifies the application of these ranges of possibilities to individual parameters or characteristics. These are divided into four categories, defined to be applicable to sound or gesture: density or rhythm of the events, tempo, timbre of sound or character of movement, and volume or size. Thus, for example, slower-faster could be applied to the rhythm of specific melodic figures and movements, or it could be interpreted in terms of the overall sense of the basic beat or pulse. Softer-louder could be interpreted in terms of the dynamic level of the sounds or the expansiveness of a dancer's gestures and movements.

The piece starts and ends in a state of consensus, labeled "equal" in the center of the diagram, involving all the performers doing something in the same way. Dancers, for example, could walk in a circle in time to a steady beat played on the same instrument by the percussionists. Underscoring Oliveros's emphasis on being attuned to those around you, the first possibility for change arises not from consciously deciding to alter your behavior, but from "perceiving" a difference that someone else is making. You can then respond according to one of four basic principles of social interaction: cooperation, conflict, independence, and competition. Thus a percussionist sensing another player starting to play more quickly could choose to cooperate by matching the new tempo, create conflict and contrast by slowing down his or her own pulse, do something completely independent by changing to complex figures on another instrument, or attempt to outdo the other musician in a competitive manner by playing still faster.

As this interaction develops, a dancer can choose to respond to what another dancer is doing, who may in turn be offering possibilities to a third dancer. These episodes of transformation are to be interspersed with periodic returns to the "equal" state. As a result, the overall sonic effect of *Traveling Companions* is a kind of texture music, marked by waves of increasing and decreasing activity where the focus is more on changes in the general categories of sound than on the specifics of individual events. The length of the work depends upon how long it takes for each of the performers to try out all eight possibilities.

MARIO DAVIDOVSKY (B. 1934)

Synchronisms No. 6 **(excerpt)**

Piece for piano and recorded electronic sounds, 1970

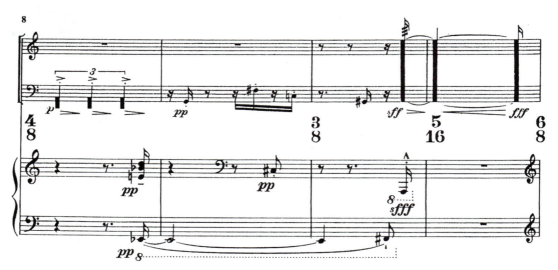

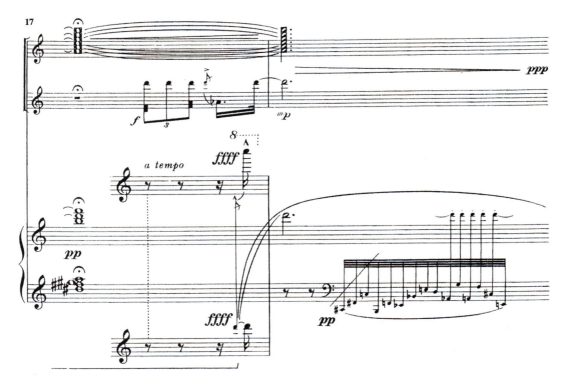

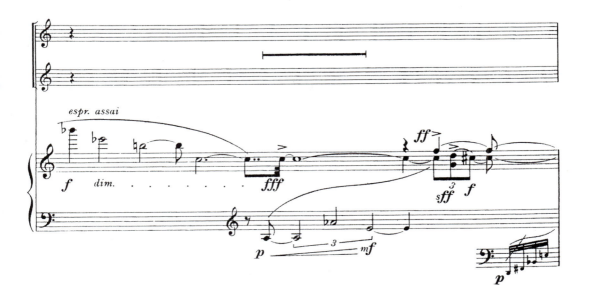

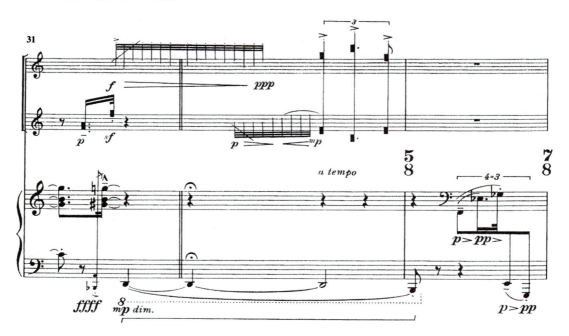

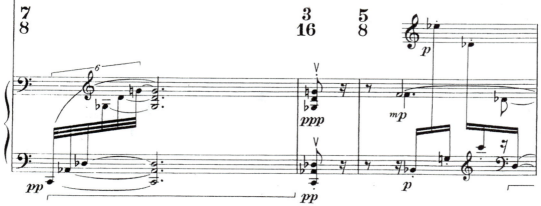

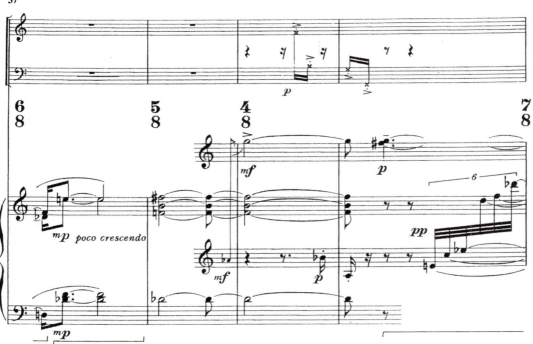

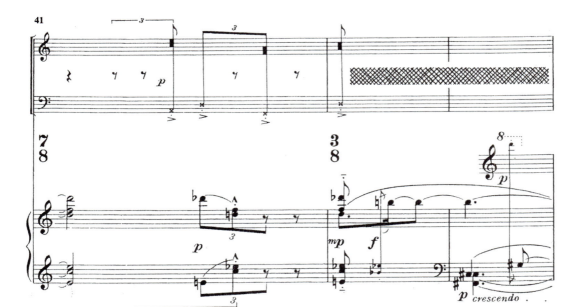

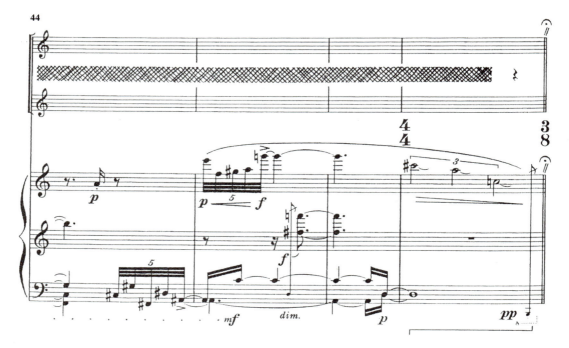

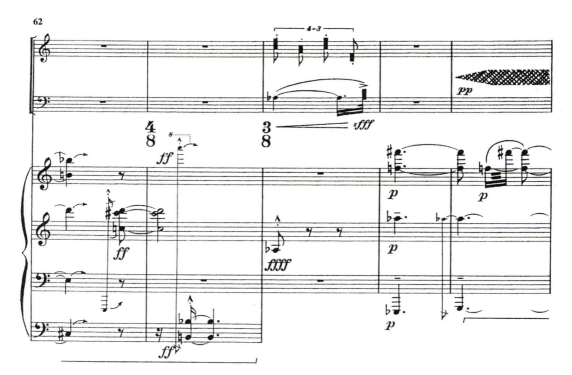

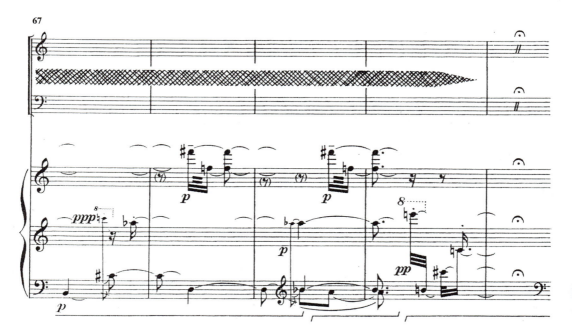

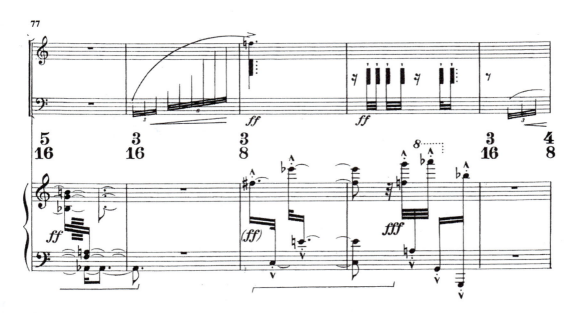

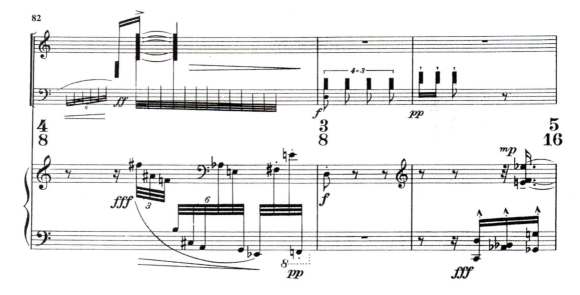

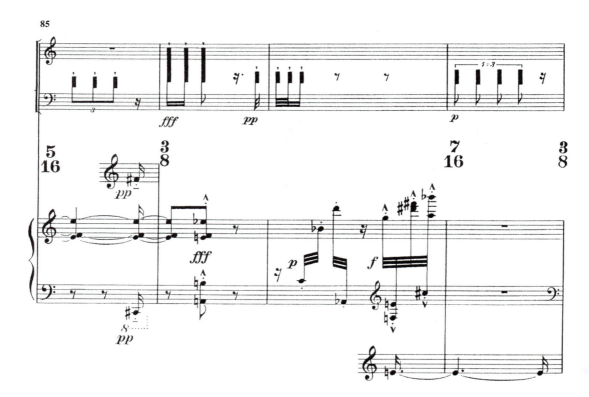

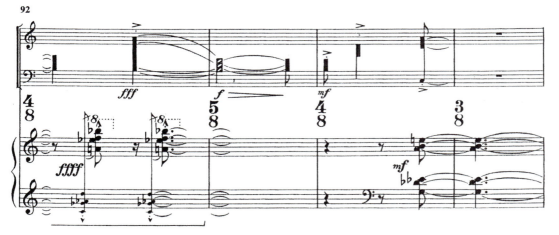

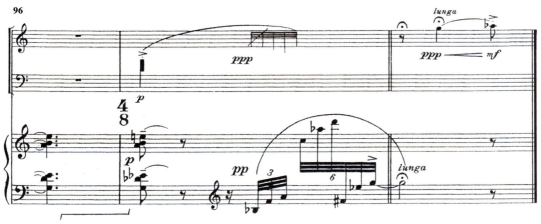

Composed at the Columbia-Princeton Electronic Music Center for the pianist Robert Miller, Davidovsky's *Synchronisms No. 6* was awarded the Pulitzer Prize in 1971. To enable the intricate interplay between the synthesized tape parts and the piano, Davidovsky specifies a high-quality stereo playback system with the two speakers placed close to the piano on either side. Although the piece is now performed using digital files, originally the electronic sounds were provided by the publisher on a reel-to-reel tape, and it remains common to refer to the electronic sounds as the tape part. Once the technician starts the tape part on a cue from the pianist, it runs without stopping until the conclusion of the work, seven minutes and ten seconds later.

As suggested by the tempo marking "♪ = 120 exactly," the success of the piece depends on the close interaction between the piano and tape, requiring the pianist to observe all tempos, rhythms, and rests precisely. In some passages the piano and electronic sounds alternate at the level of the sixteenth note (see m. 9) and later even the thirty-second note; in other places the tape part provides a textural background (as in mm. 43–48). It follows that Davidovksy notated the rhythms and dynamics of the tape part very precisely. When there are specific pitches, these are also indicated, as in measure 27, where the tape part doubles the piano. Where pitches are not specified, he uses square blocks for clusters or x-shaped noteheads for sounds with indeterminate pitch. More generalized textural passages are indicated by a thick bar with hash marks, which is as far as he goes in attempting to notate the many striking and complex timbres used throughout the piece.

Pitch does play an important role in *Synchronisms No. 6*, in particular the opening g″, which together with its distinctive timbre and dynamic envelope (see below) helps define the formal return in measure 98. While Davidovsky did not pursue strict twelve-tone composition, the overall sound world recalls the ametric pointillism of Webern's Symphony Op. 21. The piece uses a tone row and its transformations in several places: we first hear the row P⁰ in measures 1–5 (G–F♯–D♭–D–F–E–A♭–A–C–B–E♭–B♭), and there is a nearly complete retrograde R⁰ in measure 18 (starting on the b♭‴). But more generally he derives motives from portions of the row; for example, the descending gesture in the piano from the upbeat to measure 7 is derived from the reordered tetrachords of the P⁹ transposition of the row (E–D♯–B♭–B–D–C♯–F–F♯–A–G♯–C–G), although the F does not appear.

Davidovsky created the tape part by synthesizing electronic sounds and then assembling them using tape editing techniques. In several passages he foregrounds the differences between the electronic sounds and the acoustic instrument, creating a clangorous effect reminiscent of a pinball machine. But his main goal was a unified sound world. *Synchronisms No. 6* thus helps us to hear the piano from the perspective of electronic music (with its manipulations of the individual parameters of pitch, duration, dynamic envelope, and timbre). The piece begins with a tone-color melody initiated by the pianist playing a single bell-like *g″*. As it fades away, the tape part answers with the same note emerging from silence and building up to a sharp attack. The resulting aural palindrome smoothly bridges the acoustic and electronic realms.

Throughout the work, Davidovsky plays with the dynamic shapes produced by the attack and decay characteristics of the piano sound in interaction with the tape. Many passages evoke the opening effect of the crescendo or decrescendo on a sustained pitch, as in measures 6, 14, 16, and 18. We can hear extensions of this idea in measures 10–12, with the decrescendo and crescendo of a noisy electronic cluster suddenly giving way to a soft, sustained piano chord, and in measure 17, where the process is reversed, with a softly sustained piano chord morphing into an electronic sound.

Later in the piece he uses the extended technique of plucking the piano strings to create an electronic effect, further bridging the acoustic and electronic sound worlds. But more striking are the many passages (such as mm. 9–10 and 22) where, through the rapid alternation of buzzy and clicky sounds on the tape and individual notes on the piano, Davidovsky causes us to hear the piano's timbre differently, thus focusing our attention on the percussive and mechanical aspects of its sound that we have learned to ignore.

20

KAIJA SAARIAHO (B. 1952)

NoaNoa
Piece for flute and live electronics, 1992

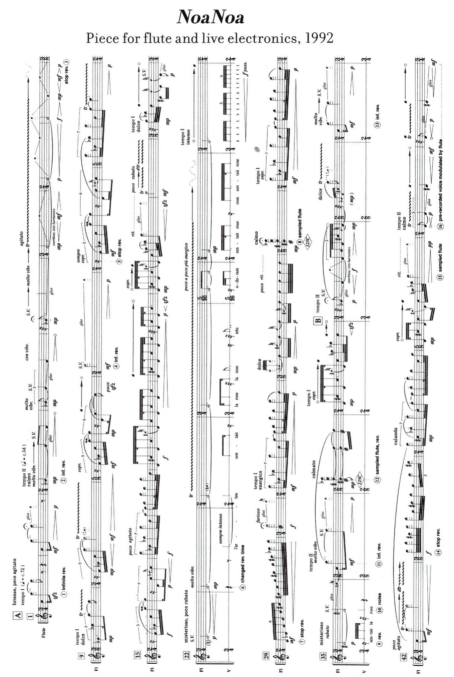

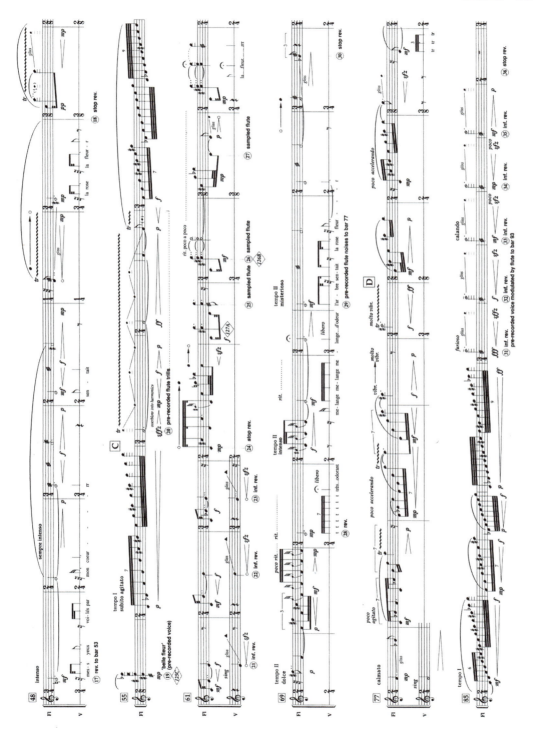

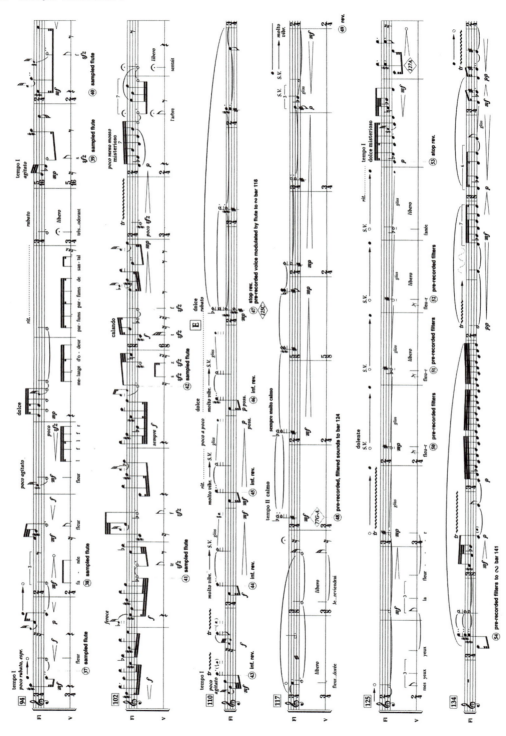

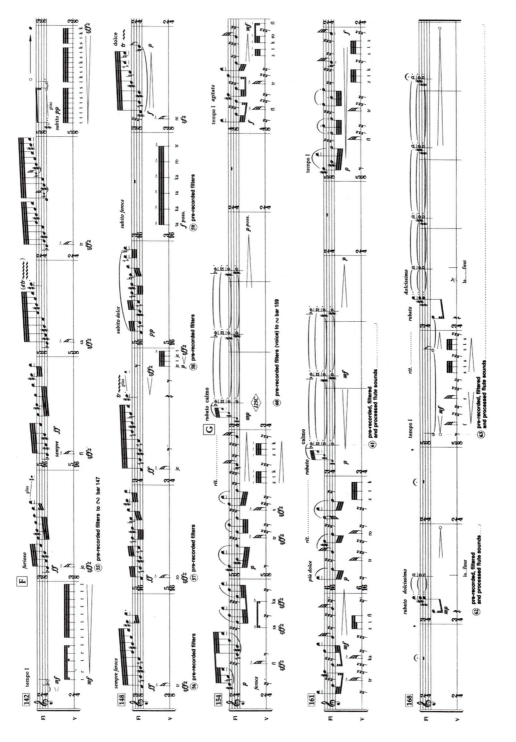

A performance of Saariaho's *NoaNoa*, for flute and interactive electronics, requires a computer with a MIDI interface, MAX software patches and samples from a CD that comes with the score or downloaded from the publisher, MIDI-controlled reverberation, and a sound system with an engineer to run it. The flutist controls the pacing of the piece by triggering the various software patches (numbered 1–63 in the score) with a foot pedal.

The title of *NoaNoa*, which is Tahitian for "fragrant," refers to a series of Primitivist woodcuts and a travel diary by the French painter Paul Gaugin from a trip he made to Tahiti at the end of the nineteenth century. Gaugin's erotically charged narrative of the beauty of the island and its inhabitants resonates in the sensuous sonic space of NoaNoa. As with Symbolist poetry, the textual fragments from Gaugin's diary—intimately whispered by the flutist or the sampled voice—emphasizes less the literal sense of the words than the sensations evoked by the words "flower," "rose," "eyes," "heart," and "perfume."

In a program note included with the score, Saariaho describes the piece as "an idea of developing several elements simultaneously, first sequentially, then superimposed on each other." We can hear this process in the contrast between the instrumental sounds of the flute and the vocal sounds produced by prerecorded samples of a male voice and by the flutist singing and speaking through the instrument. The piece was composed for the female flutist Camilla Hoitenga, whose playing is also featured in the prerecorded flute sounds. The 9-minute-long piece, with its large-scale **AA'BA''** form (charted in the table below), enacts an encounter between two forces moving from a destabilizing confrontation, through dialogue, to a powerful fusion.

SECTION	SUBSECTION	MEASURES	DESCRIPTION
A	**a**	1–21	Flute alone, developmental melody, with infinite reverb
	b	22–28	Voice with flute drone
	a'	29–40	Flute, sampled flute, agitated scales, multiphonics; one-measure vocal interpolation
A'	**a**	41–47	Flute and sampled flute, two-measure vocal interpolation
	b	48–53	Voice with flute drone, male voice
	a'	54–68	Flute, male voice, sampled flute, trills, agitated scales, vocal glissandi, multiphonics
B	**c**	69–93	Dialogues of flute and voice, flute and sampled flute, agitated scales, male voice, climax
	c'	94–109	Dialogues of flute and voice, flute and sampled flute
A''	**a**	110–124	Flute, multiphonics and bell sounds, voice and male voice

SECTION	SUBSECTION	MEASURES	DESCRIPTION
	b	125–142	Voice with flute drone, multiphonics, bell sounds
	a′	143–153	Flute and voice, agitated scales, phonemes
CODA		154–175	Interpenetrating flute and voice, multiphonics, bell sounds

Saariaho creates contrast within the three **A** sections by using an **aba′** form. The piece begins in section **a** with the flutist employing extended techniques, including microtonal inflections, noisy breath effects, and multiphonics. These sometimes delicate techniques are amplified by the "infinite reverberation" effect used at several points, which is designed so that the quieter the sound, the longer and louder the reverberation. The dramatic opening gesture of a rapid leap up from c′ to e‴ marks the returns of section a material throughout piece. The opening melody proceeds through a process of developing variation, gradually building up a nine-note collection (C–D♭–D–E♭–E–F–G♭–A–B♭). This collection is also used in the **a′** section (mm. 29–40), which includes some literal repetitions of passages from **a** (compare m. 16 to mm. 31 and 34).

In the contrasting **b** section (m. 22), the florid flute melody of the opening suddenly gives way to long, sustained tones, here and later emphasizing the pitch c′, to which is gradually added one of the many types of trills used in the work. Most important, the **b** section introduces striking vocal effects produced by the flutist speaking, whispering, and singing through instrument. Here and in the return of the **b** section in measure 48, the emphasis is on words and phrases. In the **A** and **A′** sections, the flamboyant flute material from the **a** section dominates; the short vocal **b** passage functions as an interpolation, the disruptive impact of which is suggested by the agitated character of the following **a′** passage.

The contrasting **B** section superimposes variants of the **a** and **b** material in the form of dialogues between the flute, sampled flute, voice, and sampled male voice. As the intensity of the interactions builds, we reach the main climax of the piece in measures 85–93, marked by fast ascending scales building to the high g‴–a‴.

With the concluding **A″** section, signaled by the return of the opening flute gesture and the emphasis on e‴, the **a** and **b** passages fuse together, joined by a striking new bell-like effect of multiphonics with processed vocal sounds. In the coda, the rapid alternation between the leaping flute figures and the breathy consonants completes the integration between the flute and vocal sounds.

21

GYÖRGY LIGETI (1923–2006)

Continuum

Harpsichord piece, 1968

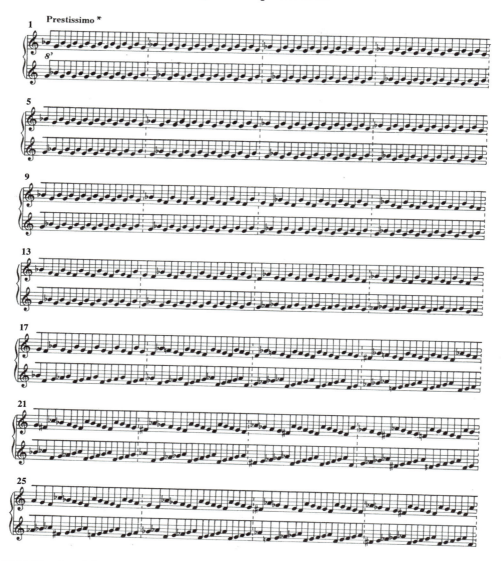

* Prestissimo = extrem schnell, so daß die Einzeltöne kaum mehr wahrzunehmen sind, sondern zu einem Kontinuum verschmelzen. Sehr gleichmäßig, ohne jede Artikulation spielen. Das richtige Tempo wurde erreicht, wenn das Stück (ohne die Schluß-Pause) weniger als vier Minuten dauert. Die vertikalen punktierten Striche sind keine Taktstriche (Takt bzw. Metrum gibt es hier nicht), sondern dienen nur zur Orientierung.

* Prestissimo = extremely fast, so that the individual tones can hardly be perceived, but rather merge into a continuum. Play very evenly, without articulation of any sort. The correct tempo has been reached when the piece lasts less than 4 minutes (not counting the long fermata at the end). The vertical broken lines are not bar lines — there is neither beat nor metre in this piece — but serve merely as a means of orientation.

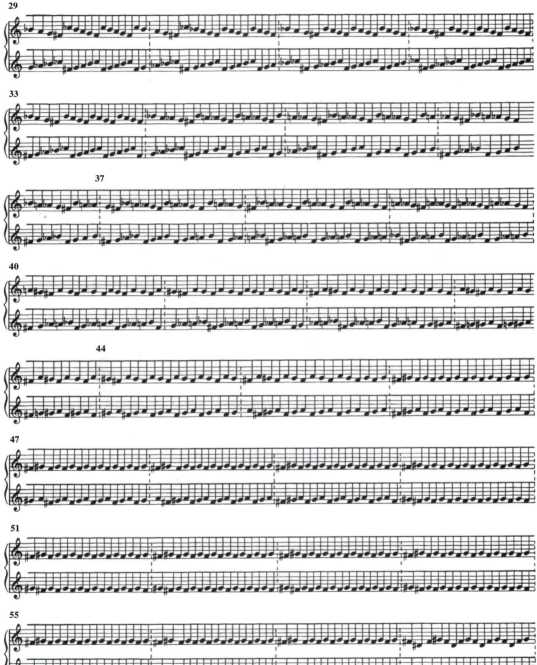

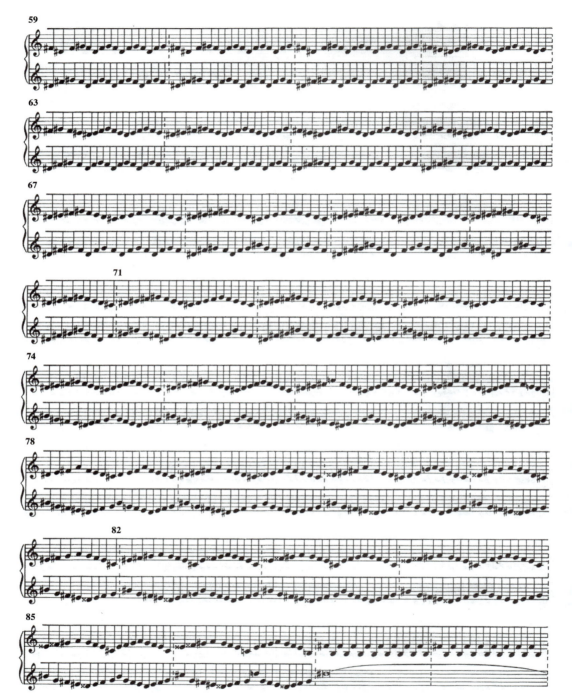

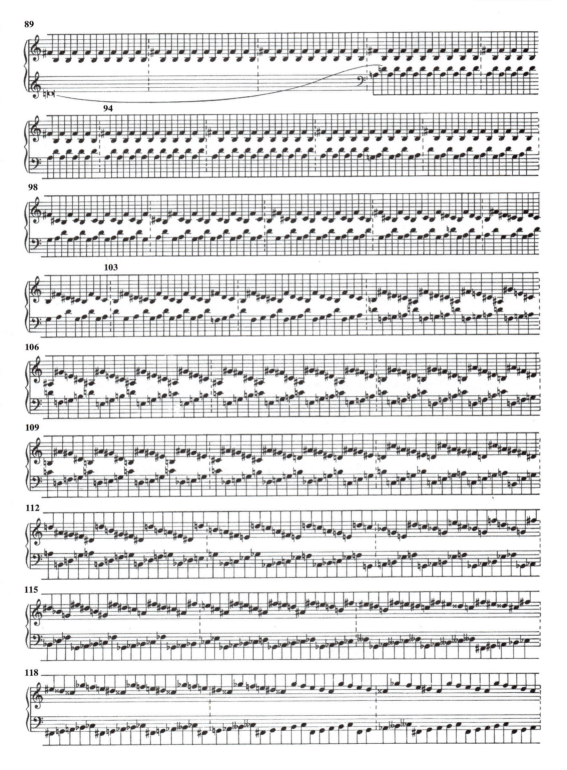

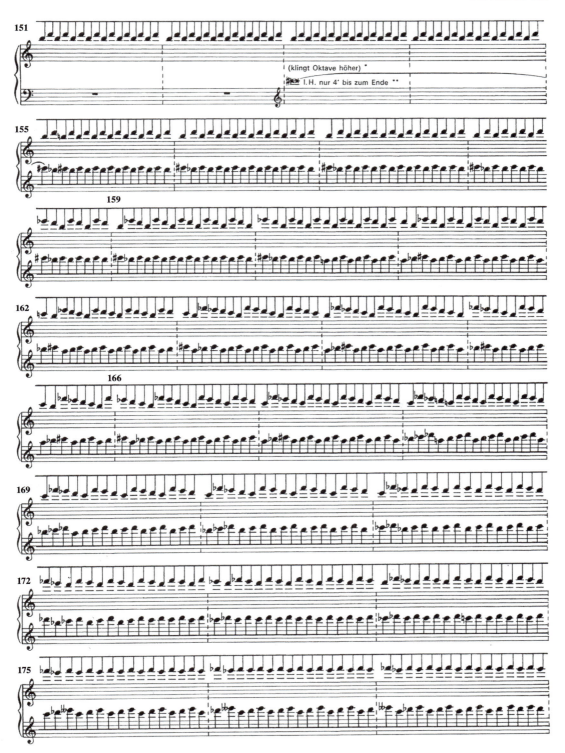

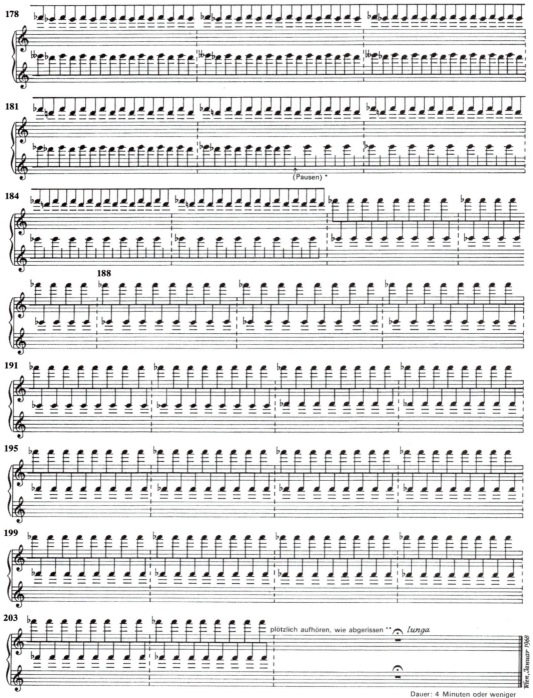

plötzlich aufhören, wie abgerissen ** lunga

Wien, Januar 1968

Dauer: 4 Minuten oder weniger
Duration: 4 minutes or less

* (rests)   ** stop suddenly, as though torn off

Ligeti composed *Continuum* on a commission from the Swiss harpsichordist Antoinette Vischer, who had pieces written for her by many other composers, including Hans Werner Henze and Luciano Berio. Vischer performed on a large, two-manual modern harpsichord with 16-foot, 8-foot, and 4-foot stops—meaning that depressing a single key would activate the pitch in three octaves, a capacity Ligeti utilizes to great dramatic effect near the end of the work.

Continuum was inspired by an experiment Ligeti heard at the Cologne Studio for Electronic Music demonstrating that a series of pitches played quickly enough would be perceived as a chord. He takes advantage of the two keyboards of the harpsichord to write very rapid overlapping passages, starting with the opening dyads (g′–b♭′ in the left hand; b♭′–g′ in the right) played as fast as possible. As he indicates in an explanatory note for the *prestissimo* tempo, the piece should be played fast enough so that it lasts 4 minutes or less; available recordings range from 3:13 to 3:41. To help orient the player, he notates the constant series of eighth notes using broken vertical lines after each series of 16, but emphasizes that they are not barlines that indicate beat or meter (we will refer to these units as "divisions.")

In *Continuum* the structures that shape the piece are right on the surface: two-note intervals, arpeggios, and scalar patterns of three, four, and five notes. At times the two hands move in tightly unified contrasting motion, but in keeping with Ligeti's imagery of a machine that is just barely holding together, they often drift out of synchronization. The development and interactions of these small patterns produce the large-scale textural effects that give *Continuum* a clear shape and direction. The shifting patterns, which in turn change the overall register and pitch content, divide the piece into five sections (as shown in Jane Piper Clendinning's analysis, given in Fig. 12.1 in *Music in the Twentieth and Twenty-First Centuries*).

Ligeti uses the speed at which the patterns change to differentiate the sections, with the opening and closing sections defined by the slowest rate of change, and internal sections evolving the most rapidly. Ligeti also varies the length of the patterns. In comparison to divisions 67–86, where we hear only two statements of a pattern per division, with the two-note patterns in divisions 1–9 and 50–55 there are eight repetitions. At the manic conclusion we hear the single note f♭′′′′ repeated 16 times in each division. Ligeti also uses the shifting patterns to vary the overall pitch content and register. Section I (divisions 1–55) is defined by the systematic expansion from the opening g′–b♭′ dyad to a chromatic cluster between f′ and c♭′, followed by a contraction to a major-second dyad of f♯′–g♯′.

While *Continuum* is not a serial piece, Ligeti carefully controls the overall pitch content. As noted earlier, the first section of the piece uses the chromatic collection between f′ and c♭′ (f′–f♯′–g′–a♭′–a′–b♭′–c♭′); in Section II he adds c′, c♯', d♯', and e'. He completes the chromatic collection with d" at the start of Section III (division 89), as the triad shifts from B major to B minor.

As the piece goes on, this cycle of making the texture thicker and more complex and then offering clarification becomes ever more dramatic. Section II (divisions 56–86) builds to the dramatic unveiling of the B-major triad, while the dense webs of Section III (divisions 87–125) suddenly open out into arpeggios as 16-foot and 4-foot stops are engaged in Section IV (divisions 126–143). At the point of widest registral expanse, Section V (divisions 143–205) unexpectedly contracts to a narrow focus on the highest register. Ligeti indicates that the sudden interruption of the frantic activity at the end of the piece is to sound "as though torn off."

22

ELLIOTT CARTER (1908–2012)

String Quartet No. 5: Introduction, Giocoso, Interlude I, Lento espressivo

String quartet, 1995

14

17

21

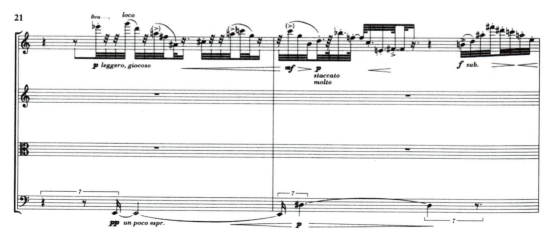

23

2. Giocoso

25 ♩ = 96

27 (⌐)

29 (⌐)

31 (⌐)

34 (⌐)

3. Interlude I

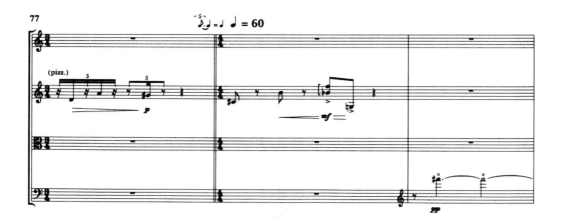

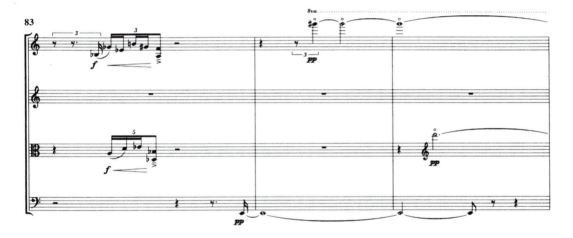

4. Lento espressivo (♩ = 60)

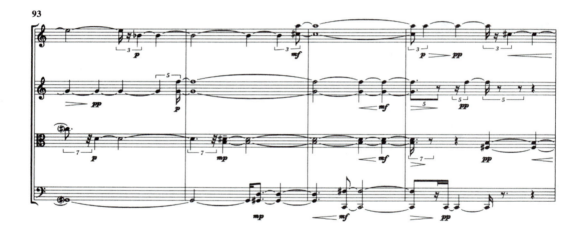

100

104

107

Elliott Carter composed his String Quartet No. 5 for the Arditti Quartet, who premiered the work in 1995. In many works Carter has treated instruments as if they were characters in a drama; he described the Quartet as capturing the lively interactions, discussions, and digressions of a chamber group rehearsing a piece. The work consists of twelve sections divided into six contrasting movements, preceded by an introduction and separated by five interludes. Carter gives each instrument a distinctive musical personality characterized by gestures, rhythm, intervallic content, and playing techniques. These sharp differentiations allow him to build up complex and shifting textures by layering the four parts in the more exploratory and diverse Introduction and Interludes, while demonstrating how each instrument takes on the mannerisms of the others to unify each of the various movements.

The Introduction establishes the personalities of the instruments along with their ways of interacting with each other. The clearest contrast is between the rough (*ruvido*) first violin, with its exclamations and exuberant flourishes, and the taciturn second violin, which for the first 16 measures limits itself to an occasional pizzicato G, sometimes with a pronounced snap where the string hits the fingerboard. Meanwhile, the subtle and restrained viola interjects soft, sustained pitches featuring harmonics and other effects, while the tender (*tenero*) cello plays lyrical lines along with longer-held notes and dyads.

Carter further differentiates the four instruments by rhythm, with duple subdivisions in the first violin, quintuplets in the second violin, triplets and sextuplets in the viola, and septuplet figures in the cello. Each instrument also draws on a distinctive repertory of intervals, as shown below. Some are unique to the instrument, while the others are shared between two of the parts, as if to provide a basis for later cooperation. Carter builds the first violin part from these intervals, with the first chord consisting of two minor sixths and a minor third, while the second chord has two minor sixths and a perfect fourth. In measures 6–7 he presents the pitches of these two chords melodically, also introducing the major second.

INTERVAL	m2	M2	m3	M3	P4	T	P5	m6	M6	m7	M7
VIOLIN I		Vn. I	Vn. I		Vn. I			Vn. I			
VIOLIN II	Vn. II		Vn. II				Vn. II			Vn. II	
VIOLA	Va.			Va.	Va.				Va.		
CELLO		Vc.				Vc.	Vc.				Vc.

The first gesture of cooperation comes in measure 10, when the viola adopts the gestural character of the first violin, which responds in turn by playing a sustained harmonic previously associated with the viola. The viola also reaches out in measure 13, reinterpreting the cello's perfect-fifth and tritone dyads from the previous two measures within its own intervallic vocabulary as a major-sixth dyad. Only the second violin refuses to cooperate, continuing obstinately with its pizzicato G until measure 17, when it finally starts to acknowledge the other instruments. This provokes a sudden outburst in measures 19–20 where all the instruments temporarily adopt the personality of the first violin, thus setting the stage for the playful movement that begins in measure 25.

In the Giocoso (humorous) all four instruments come to a consensus about how to proceed by following the lead of the first violin. While each part uses the first violin's lively and varied rhythmic motion and extended expressive melodies, they still mostly retain their characteristic rhythms and intervals. And yet Carter also shows that the instruments are able to learn from each other, as when starting in measure 47 the first violin takes on the septuplet rhythms previously associated with the cello, which in turn borrows the first violin's duple subdivisions. At the end of the Giocoso in measure 62, the viola similarly adopts the "rough" chordal exclamations with which the first violin started the work.

After the first Interlude, the Lento espressivo (slow and expressive) is a tender and contemplative chorale in which all the parts develop the sustained notes and dyads associated with the cello in the Introduction. This process of cooperation and accommodation continues in later sections; thus the viola predominates in the Adagio, which features ethereal chords in harmonics, while the second violin takes over the closing Capriccioso (capricious), with all the instruments playing pizzicato.

Carter creates continuity throughout the sections by using "tempo" or "metric modulation." For example, in measures 25–26 he broadens the tempo from $\jmath$ = 96 to $\jmath$ = 64 in the Giocoso by reinterpreting the sixteenth-note subdivision as a sixteenth-note triplet. As a result, instead of the quarter-note pulse containing four sixteenth notes as in measure 25, starting in measure 26 the slower quarter-note pulse now contains six of the same sixteenth notes. In measures 45–46 there is a small increase in tempo as the thirty-second note in measure 45 is reinterpreted as a septuplet, so that the quarter-note pulse is now defined by seven rather than eight thirty-second notes.

GEORGE CRUMB (B. 1929)

Vox balaenae: Vocalise (. . . for the beginning of time)
Chamber music, 1971

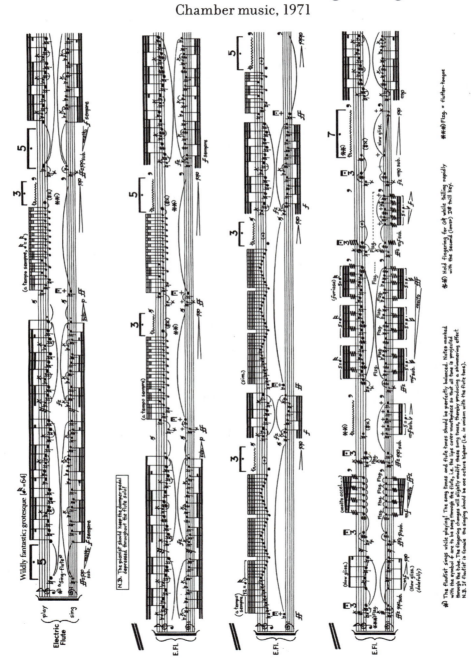

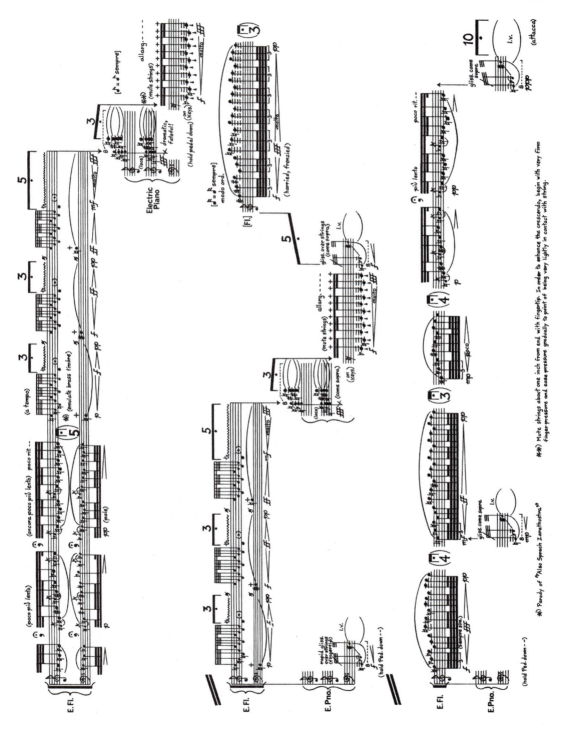

* Parody of "Also Speech Zarathustra"

***) Mute strings about one inch from end with fingertip. In order to enhance the crescendo, begin with very firm finger pressure and ease pressure gradually to point of being very lightly in contact with string.

Written in 1971 for the New York Camerata, who premiered the work the next year, *Vox balaenae* (Voice of the Whale) calls for flute, cello, and piano. Crumb indicates that the instruments are to be amplified, which produces a powerful effect in the loud passages while making the piece's many delicate extended techniques more audible. Crumb was inspired to compose the piece after hearing some of the first recordings of the songs of the humpback whale. Over the three continuous movements he charts the vast span of time that whales have existed, including up to the era of mankind, and the present-day threats to their continuing survival.

The most immediately striking aspect of *Vox balaenae* is the extraordinary sound world that Crumb captures through his meticulously notated score and three pages of performance directions. Special techniques for the piano include strumming or muting the strings and the use of preparations, such as a chisel, paper clips, and a glass rod. For the cello, Crumb specifies that it be retuned to allow the open-string B dominant seventh featured in the theme and variations of the second movement; he creates a "seagull effect" in "Archeozoic" (Variation 1) by a glissando in harmonics. In the performance directions he also specifies theatrical aspects, including deep-blue stage lighting to intensify the work's mystical oceanic atmosphere and black half masks for the musicians, which "by effacing the sense of human projection, are intended to represent, symbolically, the powerful impersonal forces of nature (i.e. nature dehumanized)."

The opening section, *Vocalise* (. . . *for the beginning of time*), directly evokes the sound of whale songs with the flutist singing through the instrument while playing. Crumb evokes timelessness through a static, nondevelopmental melody reminiscent of the highly ornamented style of the Japanese shakuhachi flute, including rapid repeated-note figures, pitch bending, and frequent grace notes. In most of the piece Crumb indicates a flexible tempo, with longer values indicated by brackets showing the approximate number of seconds (thus the opening d′ is to be sustained approximately five seconds). This contemplative passage is interrupted by what Crumb described as a parody of the opening of Richard Strauss's *Also sprach Zarathustra*. In Strauss's symphonic poem, this music, with its rising trumpet call c′–g′–c″ and dramatic alternation of C-major and C-minor triads, represents the triumphant emergence of Nietzsche's "Superman." Here Crumb uses the tritone to transform it into a more menacing intrusion to illustrate mankind's disruption of the natural world.

The *Zarathustra* quote provides much of the harmonic and melodic material of the piece. The two tritone-related major and minor triads (F major, B minor; F minor, B major) comprise the octatonic collection (F–F♯–A♭–A–B–C–D–D♯), with its characteristic alternation of half steps and whole steps. In some passages Crumb foregrounds the octatonic collection, as in the flute passage that follows the quotation (A♯–[C]–C♯–D♯–E–[F♯]–G–A). He then transposes the flute passage down five half steps three times (measured from the starting pitches A♯–F–C–G), thus taking us through the three versions of the octatonic collection.

But more commonly Crumb combines octatonic and diatonic elements. He makes this technique audible in the further development of the flute melody: at what would have been the fourth transposition (down to D), we return instead to the opening *Vocalise*. This material is not strictly octatonic but has a generalized "exotic" quality that suggests both Middle Eastern and Asian modes (D–E–F–A♭–A–B♭–B).

CHEN YI (B. 1953)

Ba Ban
Piano piece, 1999

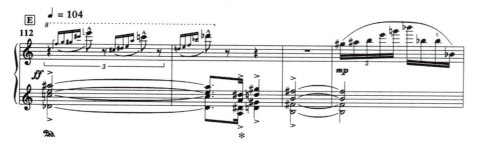

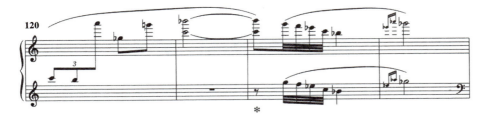

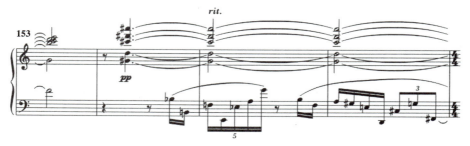

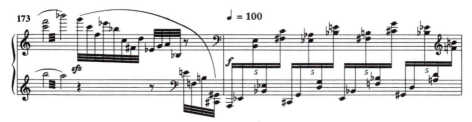

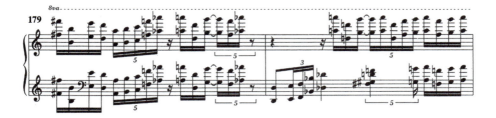

Composed as part of a Carnegie Hall commission for new piano works to celebrate the millennium, Chen Yi's *Ba Ban* integrates compositional elements from her native China along with twelve-tone techniques and a virtuosic piano style evoking Béla Bartók and Olivier Messiaen. Chen based the work on a centuries-old Chinese instrumental piece called *Ba Ban*, literally "eight beats." Using half-step grace notes to imitate bright cymbals and low gongs, she begins with the opening pitches of the pentatonic *Ba Ban* melody divided between the two hands, spelled as in the original piece: Bb–Bb–Eb–Ab–F♯; C♯–D♯–F♯; Eb–F♯–Bb–Ab. These three motives from the theme reappear throughout the work.

The original tune consists of eight phrases that follow a pattern of beats given in measures 239–253. Chen presents the *Ba Ban* pattern using groups of eighth-note triplets on the top C of the piano, with the start of each phrase signaled by a grace note: 3 + 2 + 3, 3 + 2 + 3, 4 + 4, 3 + 2 + 3, 3 + 2 + 3 + 2 + 2, 4 + 4, 5 + 3, and 4 + 4. Each of the eight phrases contains eight beats, except for the fifth, which is extended by four beats, corresponding to the golden section, a mathematical ratio important to Chinese numerology and aesthetics.

Chen builds on this structure by organizing the piece in eight sections (labeled A–H in the score), which she compares to a sectional form used in Chinese folk music that presents a theme with changing ornamentation, tempos, and performance techniques. She also describes *Ba Ban* as a theme and three variations, followed by a coda. The eight-part form is further complicated by two large-scale repetitions, with measures 50–63 and 76–97 reworked and transposed in measures 98–111 and 124–144.

THEME	Theme	Transition	Var. 1	Var. 2	Transition	Var. 3		Coda
FIRST MEASURE	1	48	64	98	112	157	184	233
SECTION	A	B	C	D	E	F	G	H

Along with the Chinese materials, the pitch structure of *Ba Ban* employs a twelve-tone row and its transpositions (B–F–C♯–D–F♯–G♯–A–D♯–E–Bb–G–C), with most statements identifiable by the distinctive opening tritone. Chen also generates melodies and harmonies from a pentachord (Bb–C–C♯–F♯–A) and its transpositions, often presented with the ascending intervallic sequence of a major second, minor second, perfect fourth, and minor third.

Both the twelve-tone row and the pentachord emerge only gradually, as if growing out of the *Ba Ban* theme. Indeed, we first hear a fragment of the row (the first eight pitches of P^0) in measure 16, in the ornamental flourish. The first complete statement of P^0 appears in the bass in measures 62–63. Chen similarly alludes to portions of the pentachord in measures 14–15, while withholding its complete form until measures 43–44 (A–B–C–F–Ab) and as a chord in the left hand of measure 48.

Over the course of the work Chen uses the *Ba Ban* theme, the row, and the pentachord singly and in various combinations. For example, the C section, Variation 1, begins in measures 64–66 with chords generated from linear segments of P^0 (B–F–C♯–D; E–B♭; A–E♭; G–C: order numbers in the row 0123; 89; 67; 10 11) arranged to produce a transposition of the opening *Ba Ban* motive in the top voice (B–E–A–G). Section F, Variation 3, features overlapping versions of the pentachord (A–B–C–F–A♭; A♭–B♭–B–E–G) that build up to a statement of P^0 (mm. 160–161) with order numbers 1234 (F–C♯–D–F♯) in the chord. This section concludes with a virtuosic passage that emphasizes the pentachord and the *Ba Ban* motives (mm. 174–183).

Chen further integrates the three types of pitch material in the driving, toccata-like Section G, which gradually unfolds the pitches of P^0 against a pedal based on its first note, B (F–C♯–D [mm. 185–186]; F♯–G♯–A–D♯ [mm. 188–189]; E–B♭–G–C [mm. 190–191]). Between these measures, with their accented syncopated notes from the row, the first four pitches of the pentachord slip in more discretely (B♭, C [m. 187]; C♯, F♯ [m. 189]). Starting in measure 193, an ostinato figure using the first six pitches of P^1 accompanies spiky versions of the *Ba Ban* motives. In a striking synthesis, Chen then transposes the ostinato to begin on C–D–E♭–A♭, and B (P^1, P^3, P^4, P^9, P^0), which thus comprises a large-scale unfolding of the pentachord to control the row structure (mm. 193–221).

The merging of Chinese and Western techniques reaches its peak in the coda, section H, where all of the elements appear in their clearest form. It begins in measure 233 with three statements of P^{10}, continues with the passage discussed earlier distilling the *Ba Ban* rhythm, and concludes with a closing gesture like elegant Chinese calligraphy that combines four statements of the pentachord with the opening *Ba Ban* motive.

STEVE REICH (B. 1936)

Violin Phase (excerpt)

Piece for violin and recorded violins, or four violins, 1967

♩ = ca. 144

Repeat each bar approximately number of times written. / Jeder Takt soll approximativ wiederholt werden entsprechend der angegebenen Anzahl. / Répétez chaque mesure à peu près le nombre de fois indiqué

Violin Phase builds on the phase-shifting technique and its remarkable psychoacoustic by-products. All the melodies, harmonies, rhythms, and textures that we hear over the five sections of the piece grow out of the opening 12-beat loop as it is combined with itself in different ways through the phasing process. As Reich discusses in the extensive directions that accompany the score, *Violin Phase* can be performed by four violins or by one violin with a prerecorded tape; it is now commonly performed with the assistance of digital samplers or computer music software.

The form of *Violin Phase* emphasizes the clarity and perceptibility of the musical processes Reich employs. Over the course of the five sections of the work, which usually lasts between 14 and 16 minutes, Reich gradually increases the number of layers from one to four, while combining the basic techniques in different ways. The score excerpt includes measures 1–19.

SECTION	COMMENTS
Section 1, mm. 1–6	Violins 1 and 2: gradual phasing process
Section 2, mm. 7–11	Violins 1, 2, 3: violin 2 plays three different resultant patterns
Section 3, mm. 12–16	Violins 1, 2, 3: gradual phasing process
Section 4, mm. 17–22	Violins 1, 2, 3, 4: violin 2 plays three different resultant patterns, each time with a gradual phasing process
Section 5, m. 23	Violins 1, 2, 3, 4: violin 2 plays a longer resultant pattern, then rejoins violin 1

Section 1 focuses on the basic phasing process, as violin 2 (the lead instrument throughout) first doubles the loop played live or on tape by violin 1, then gradually speeds up until it is one eighth note ahead at measure 3. As the phasing process begins, you hear a slight echo effect, then more of a delay, and then complex rhythms as the two loops pull further apart. Once violin 2 reaches measure 3, the player holds the tempo to sustain the relationship for between eight and sixteen repetitions, enough to establish the aural clarity of the out-of-phase loops. Then the gradual process continues, with violin 2 moving ahead two eighth notes (m. 4), then three eighth notes (m. 5), and finally four eighth notes (m. 6).

Section 2 begins when violin 3 (live or on tape) takes over playing the out-of-phase loop from violin 2. Starting in measure 9, violin 2 plays resultant patterns produced by the out-of-phase loops. In the fourth stave, Reich notates three patterns, beginning with a one-measure rhythmic alternation between the perfect-fourth and fifth dyad, emphasizing the high e″. In what he describes as a three-stage "pointing out process," the violinist very softly starts to play a resultant pattern with a gradual crescendo (m. 9). Reaching *forte*, the pattern is repeated four to six times (m. 9a). The violinist then slowly fades back out (m. 9b), so that the pattern continues to sound in the listener's ear. The resultant pattern in measure 10 is an ostinato figure emphasizing the low c♯′, while measure 11 introduces a lyrical two-measure folklike melody. The blank staff at the bottom starting in measure 9 is provided for the violinist to come up with his or her own patterns.

Reich repeats the phasing process with a third layer of the basic loop added in section 3. In section 4, violin 2 plays patterns created by the other three parts, while also speeding up to create phase shifting. Section 5 features another extended resultant pattern.

The richness of the music resulting from these phasing processes depends on the rhythmic and pitch structure of the basic loop. Reich has devised a loop that offers both melodic and harmonic material, including the prominent repeating melodic strand in the lower register (c♯′–f♯′–a′–g♯′–b′) and the perfect fifths and fourths in the upper register (a′–e″; b′–e″). These six pitches sustain the listener's interest because of the tonal ambiguity of the basic collection: c♯′–f♯′–g♯′–a′–b′–e″, with its implications of F♯ minor, F♯ Dorian, and A major, depending on which pitches are emphasized.

As the piece continues and more layers are added, the triadic implications of the loop are deemphasized in favor of 025 and 027 pitch-class sets (consisting of a major second and either a perfect fourth or perfect fifth). The four-note chords that dominate sections 3, 4, and 5 emphasize stacked perfect fourths (c♯′–f♯′–b′–e″).

Reflecting Reich's studies of West African music, the rhythmic structure of *Violin Phase* builds on the metric ambiguities of the 12-beat bell pattern of Ewe music. The basic loop consists of two statements of a figure that is five eighth notes long; the statements are placed asymmetrically in the 12-beat measure, the first starting on the downbeat, the second starting on the weak eighth beat. As the phasing process begins, each new configuration shifts the perceived downbeat, and thus unsettles all the other pitch and metric hierarchies in stimulating ways.

JOHN ADAMS (B. 1947)

Doctor Atomic, Act 1, Scene 3, *Batter my heart*

Opera, 2005

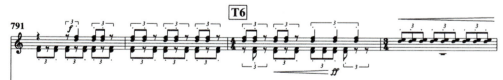

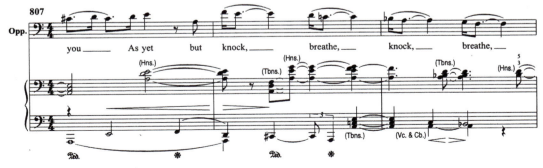

knock, _ breathe, _ shine, _ and _ seek to mend; ___ Bat-ter ___ my heart, ___

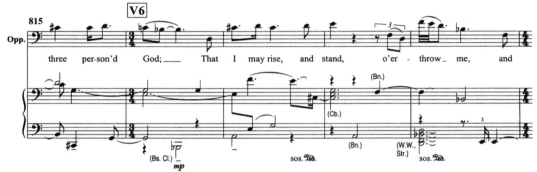

three per-son'd God; ___ That I may rise, and stand, o'er - throw _ me, and

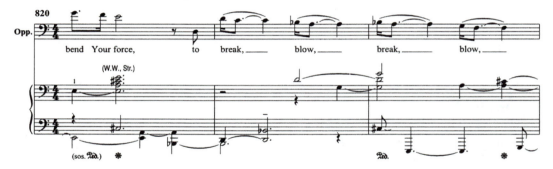

bend Your force, to break, ___ blow, ___ break, ___ blow, ___

break, ___ blow, ___ burn _ and _ make me new. ___

*Upbeat to m.831 – downbeat of m.838: for fuller sonority on piano, L.H. may play one octave lower.

845

Opp.

knock, breathe, shine, and seek to mend; Bat-ter my heart,

850

Opp.

three per-son'd God; That I may rise, and stand, o'er - throw me, and

855

Opp.

bend Your force, to break, blow, break, blow,

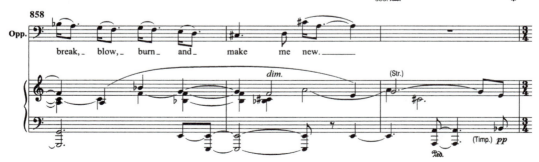

858

Opp.

break, blow, burn and make me new.

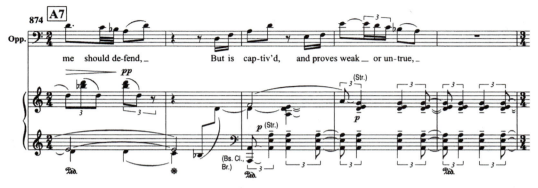

me should de-fend,___ But is cap-tiv'd, and proves weak ___ or un-true,___

Yet dear-ly'_____ I love you,_ and would be_ lov'd_ fain,_____

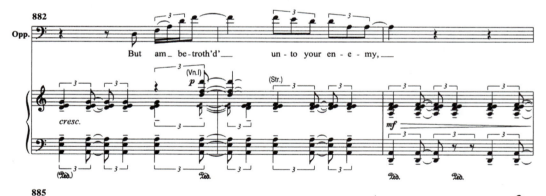

But am _ be-troth'd'____ un-to your en-e-my,

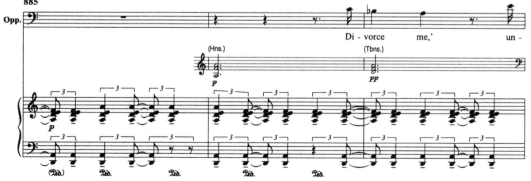

Di-vorce me,' un-

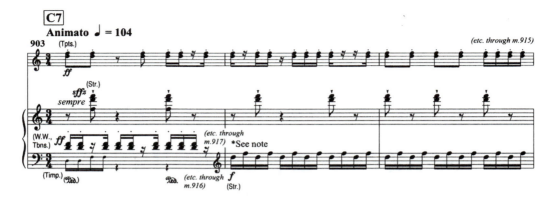

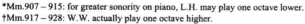

*Mm.907 – 915: for greater sonority on piano, L.H. may play one octave lower.
†Mm.917 – 928: W.W. actually play one octave higher.

End of Act One

Batter my heart, three-person'd God, for you
As yet but knock, breathe, shine, and seek to mend;
(Batter my heart, three-person'd God,)
That I may rise, and stand, o'erthrow me, and bend
Your force, to break, blow, burn, and make me new.

(Batter my heart, three-person'd God, for you
As yet but knock, breathe, shine, and seek to mend;
Batter my heart, three-person'd God,
That I may rise, and stand, o'erthrow me, and bend
Your force, to break, blow, burn, and make me new.)

I, like an usurpt town, to another due,
Labour to admit you, but Oh, to no end.
Reason, your viceroy in me, me should defend,
But is captiv'd, and proves weak or untrue.

Yet dearly I love you, and would be lov'd fain,
But am betroth'd unto your enemy;
Divorce me, untie, or break that knot again,
Take me to you, imprison me, for I,
Except you enthrall me, never shall be free,
Nor ever chaste, except you ravish me.

❧❦❧

John Adams's *Doctor Atomic* presents the physicist J. Robert Oppenheimer in the intensive final stages of the Manhattan Project at Los Alamos, New Mexico, leading up to the detonation of the first atomic bomb in the summer of 1945. Act 1, scene 3 takes place the night before the detonation, as a violent electrical storm breaks out unexpectedly at the test site where the scientists are gathered, shattering everyone's nerves with fears of having to cancel the blast, as well as concerns that the bomb could be set off prematurely. In the midst of the panic and chaos, Oppenheimer's aria "Batter my heart" captures a moment of solitude in which he expresses his anguished internal struggles about the project.

"Batter my heart" is based on a sonnet by the seventeenth-century English poet John Donne that inspired Oppenheimer to name the atomic test site "Trinity." Donne's poem uses powerfully sensuous language to capture a struggle between the desires of the self and flesh and a longing to give oneself over to the Trinity of the Father, the Son, and the Holy Spirit. The aria expresses a similar internal struggle that Oppenheimer feels between good and evil, darkness and light, as he is bringing forth this new weapon.

Oppenheimer seems to address both God and the bomb itself as he grapples with the terrible seduction of unleashing the godlike powers of the bomb to "shine . . . break, blow, burn."

Adams uses textual repetitions (indicated in parentheses in the text given on the previous page) to restructure Donne's 14-line sonnet into an **AAB** form. The vocal sections are framed by extended instrumental passages, with a shorter instrumental interpolation after the first **A** section. While the vocal passages evoke seventeenth-century music, the instrumental sections are based on Minimalist techniques, thus illustrating the eclectic combination of elements typical of Postminimalism. The opening instrumental passage features an accumulation of layers based on a D–F dyad, using Adams's distinctive fast syncopated rhythms to depict Oppenheimer's agitation. In keeping with his interest in reconnecting with tonality, Adams gradually introduces the elements of a first-inversion dominant (mm. 794–795) that moves to a D-minor triad to end the section (m. 801).

FORM	X	A		X′	A′		B			X″
SECTION		a	a′		a	a′	b	c	d	
FIRST MEASURE	767	802	813	826	836	848	861	872	887	903
TEXT		Batter my heart . . .	Batter my heart . . .		Batter my heart . . .	Batter my heart . . .	I, like an usurpt town . . .	Reason, your viceroy . . .	Divorce me . . .	

In the vocal passages Adams adapts features of the chaconne, a variation form developed in the sixteenth and seventeenth centuries based on a sequence of chords and a repeating bass line. We hear the clearest version of the chaconne material in the brass and winds in measures 886–892, but it is also foregrounded in measures 811–815 and 846–850. Adams emphasizes the tonal implications of the chaconne material at several points, creating a strong sense of D minor via progressions from submediant to dominant to tonic—in measures 819–820, measures 854–55, and throughout the contrasting passage in the **B** section, measures 861–902.

But Adams also uses the descending melody of the chaconne in passages without a triadic orientation to generate bass lines and vocal melodies. Thus, for example, the pitches we hear in the accompaniment in measures 889–891 (F–E–D–C–B♭) are related to the long descending melody in measures 808–811 and 821–824 (F–E–D–C–B♭–A–G–F–E–D–C♯–D), corresponding to the key lines "knock, breathe, shine," and "break, blow, burn" and their many repetitions in the aria. Adams uses portions of this descending line at several points in different registers, such as in the bass at the beginning of the vocal section in measures 802–806 (F–E–D–C♯). Much of the vocal melody is similarly derived from the descending line, as in the setting of the words "Batter my heart" (C–B♭–A–G), and in the expressive ornamental figures such as for "o'er-throw-me" in measure 819 (F–E–D–B♭). The dyads of the instrumental passages (D–F; D–E; C♯–E) are also generated from the conclusion of the descending line (F–E–D–C♯–D), which can thus be heard as a sort of nucleus for the entire aria.

◉ Norton Opera Sampler video available

READING AN ORCHESTRAL SCORE

CLEFS

The music for some instruments is written in clefs other than the familiar treble and bass. In the following example, middle C is shown in the four clefs used in orchestral scores:

The alto clef is primarily used in viola parts. The tenor clef is employed for cello, bassoon, and trombone parts when these instruments play in a high register.

TRANSPOSING INSTRUMENTS

The music for some instruments is customarily written at a pitch different from their actual sound. The following list, with examples, shows the transposing instruments that appear in this volume.

Instrument	Transposition	Written note	Actual sound
Celesta Piccolo	sound an octave higher than written		
Trumpet in F	sounds a perfect fourth higher than written		
Clarinet in E♭	sounds a minor third higher than written		
Piccolo trumpet in D Clarinet in D	sound a major second higher than written		
Clarinet in B♭	sounds a major second lower than written		
Clarinet in A	sounds a minor third lower than written		
Flute in G	sounds a perfect fourth lower than written		
English horn Horn in F	sound a perfect fifth lower than written		
Contrabassoon Double bass Guitar	sound an octave lower than written		
Bass clarinet in B♭ (written in treble clef)	sounds a major ninth lower than written		

INSTRUMENT NAMES AND ABBREVIATIONS

WOODWINDS

English	French	German	Italian
Piccolo (Picc.)	Petite flûte (Pte. fl.)	Kleine Flöte (Kl. Fl.), Pikkolo (Pik.)	Flauto piccolo (Fl. picc.)
Flute (Fl.)	Flûte (Fl.)	Flöte (Fl.)	Flauto grande (Fl. gr.), Flauto (Fl.)
Alto flute (Alto fl.)	Flûte alto (Fl. alto)	Altflöte (Altfl.)	Flauto alto (Fl. alto)
Oboe (Ob.)	Hautbois (Hb.)	Oboe (Ob.)	Oboe (Ob.)
English horn (E.H.)	Cor anglais (C.a.)	Englisch Horn (E.H., Engl. Hr.)	Corno inglese (C.I., C. ing.)
Clarinet in E♭ (E♭ cl.), Clarinet in D (D cl.)	Petite clarinette (Pte. cl.)	Klarinette in Es (Es Kl.), Klarinette in D (D Kl.)	Clarinetto Piccolo (Cl. picc.)
Clarinet (Cl., Clar.)	Clarinette (Cl.)	Klarinette (Kl.)	Clarinetto (Cl.)
Bass clarinet (Bs. Cl.)	Clarinette basse (Cl. bs.)	Baβklarinette (Bkl., Bs. Kl.)	Clarinetto basso (Cl. bas.)
Bassoon (Bn., Bsn.)	Basson (Bssn.)	Fagott (Fag.)	Fagotto (Fag.)
Contrabassoon (C. bsn.)	Contrebasson (C. bssn.)	Kontrafagott (K. fag.)	Contrafagotto (Cfg.)

BRASS

English	French	German	Italian
Horn (Hn., Hr.)	Cor	Horn (Hr., Hrn.)	Corno (Cor.)
Piccolo trumpet (P. tpt.)	Petite trompette (Pte. tr.)	Trompete in D (D Trp.)	Tromba piccola (Tr. picc., Trba. picc.)
Trumpet (Tpt., Trpt.)	Trompette (Tr.)	Trompete (Trmp., Trp.)	Tromba (Trba.)
Trombone (Tbn., Trb.)	Trombone (Tr.)	Posaune (Pos.)	Trombone (Trne.)
Bass trombone (B. trb.)	Trombone basse (Tr. bs.)	Baβposaune (B. Pos.)	Trombone basso (Trne. basso)
Tuba (Tb.)	Tuba (Tb.)	Tuba (Tub.), Kontrabaβtuba (Kbt.)	Tuba (Tb.)

PERCUSSION

English	French	German	Italian
Kettledrums (K.D.), Timpani (Timp.)	Timbales (Timb.)	Pauken (Pke.)	Timpani (Timp.)
Sleigh bells (Sleigh b.)	Grelots	Schellen	Sonagli (Son.)
Snare drum (Sn. Drum)	Caisse Claire (C. cl.)	Kleine Trommel (Kl. Tr.)	Tamburo militaire (Tamb. milit.)
Cymbals (Cym., Cymb.)	Cymbales (Cym.)	Becken (Beck.)	Piatti (P.)
Bass drum (B.D., B. Drum)	Grosse caisse (Gr. c.)	Groβe Trommel (Gr. Tromm.)	Gran cassa (Gr. cassa)
Triangle (Trgl.)	Triangle (Triang.)	Triangel (Tgl.)	Triangolo (Trgl.)

STRINGS

English	French	German	Italian
Violin (Vl., Vn.)	Violon (V.)	Geige (G., Gg.), Violine (Viol.)	Violino (Vl.)
Viola (Va., Vla.)	Alto (A.)	Bratsche (Br.), Viola (Vla.)	Viola (Vle.)
Violoncello, Cello (Vc., Vlc.)	Violoncelle (Vc.)	Violoncell (Vcl., Vlc.)	Violoncello (Vc., Vlc.)
Double bass (D. bs.), Contrabass (Cb.)	Contrebasse (C.B.)	Kontrabaβ (K. Bs.), Contrabass (Cb.)	Contrabasso (Cb.)

OTHER INSTRUMENTS

English	French	German	Italian
Harp (Hp.)	Harpe (Hp.)	Harfe (Hfe., Hrf.)	Arpa (A.)
Guitar (Gtr.)	Guitare (Guit.)	Gitarre (Git.)	Chitarra
Piano (Pno.)	Piano	Klavier	Pianoforte (Pft.)
Upright piano		Pianino	
Organ (Org.)	Orgue (Org.)	Orgel (Org.)	Organo (Org.)
Celesta (Cel.)	Célesta (Cél.)	Celesta (Cel.)	Celesta (Cel.)

NOTE NAMES

English	French	German	Italian
C	ut	C	do
C♯	ut dièse	Cis	do diesis
D♭	ré bémol	Des	re bemolle
D	ré	D	re
D♯	ré dièse	Dis	re diesis
E♭	mi bémol	Es	mi bemolle
E	mi	E	mi
E♯	mi dièse	Eis	mi diesis
F♭	fa bémol	Fes	fa bemolle
F	fa	F	fa
F♯	fa dièse	Fis	fa diesis
G♭	sol bémol	Ges	sol bemolle
G	sol	G	sol
G♯	sol dièse	Gis	sol diesis
A♭	la bémol	As	la bemolle
A	la	A	la
A♯	la dièse	Ais	la diesis
B♭	si bémol	B	si bemolle
B	si	H	si
B♯	si dièse	His	si diesis
C♭	ut bémol	Ces	do bemolle

GLOSSARY OF PERFORMANCE INDICATIONS

3fach *see* dreifach

a at, by

ab off

abdämpfen to mute

aber but

accelerando (accel.) becoming faster

ad libitum (ad lib.) at the performer's choice

agitato agitated, excited

allargando becoming slower and broader

allegramente cheerfully

allegretto a moderately fast tempo

allegro a rapid tempo

allein alone

allmählig gradual

also thus

am, an on

ancora once more

andante a moderately slow tempo

Anfang beginning

animato animated

animé, animez becoming faster, lively

Anmerkung comment

archet to bow

arco played with the bow

arrêt pause

articulato articulated

assai very

assez quite

au to

auf on, to

aussi as

Ausdruck expression

Ausnahme exception

äußerst extremely

avec with

beaucoup very much

beide both

ben well

bewegt agitated

Bewegung motion

bis until

bleibt stays

bref short

breit broad

brillante brilliant

cadenza a solo passage in an improvisational style

calando gradually diminishing

calmato quieting, quieted

calmo calm, quiet

cantabile (cant.) singable, songlike

cantando (cant.) singing

chevalet bridge

claire clear

col, colla (coll') with the

col canto, colla voce following the soloist

come like, as

con with

cordes strings

court short

cuivré brassy, resonant

Dämpfer (Dpf.) mute

dans in

davantage more

dehors outside

dessus treble

diminuendo (dim., dimin.) becoming softer

Dirigent conductor

dirigiren (dirigieren) to direct

divisi (div.) divided

dolce sweetly

dolente sorrowful

dreifach (3fach) in threes

droite right

durch through

durchaus throughout

eco echo

eilen hurry, rush

Einsatz entry

en to

encore again

erst first

espressivo (espr., espress.) expressive

etwas somewhat

feroce fierce

Flageolett (Flag.) harmonic

Flatterzunge (Fltz., Flttz., Flzg.) flutter-tongue

flüchtig fleeting

fortlaufend continuous

für for

furioso raging

ganz whole

Ganzton whole step

gauche left

gedämpft muted

geheimnisvoll full of mystery

geschlagen struck

gespielt played

gestopft (gest.) stopped

getheilt (geth.) divided

giocoso playful, humorous

gleichmässig even

glissando slide between pitches

graziosamente gracefully

Griffbrett fingerboard

große Pause (G. P.) long pause

Halbe half note

Halbton half step

Hälfte half

Halt stop

heftig heavy

hervor forth

hervortreten stand out

hinaufziehen pull up

hoch high

höher higher

immer always

jeu play

kein no

klingt sounds

kurz short

laissez let

lange long

langhallend long-reverberating

langsam slow

large broad

lassen let

lebhaft lively

legato (leg.) smooth

leggierto (legg.) lightly

legno wood

leise soft

loco at normal pitch

lenteur slowness

lento a slow tempo

letzte last
libero free
liegen lie, rest
lunga long
m. d. (main droite) right hand
m. g. (main gauche) left hand
maestoso majestic
main hand
marcato (marc.) with emphasis
marschmäßig march-like
martellato hammered, strongly marked
mässig moderate
meno less
misterioso mysterious
mit with
moderato at a moderate tempo
modérément moderate
modo manner, way
molto very much
morendo dying away
mosso rapid
moto motion
muta change
nachgeben to ease off
nach und nach gradually
Naturlaut sound of nature
neu new
nicht not
offen open
ohne (o.) without
ongles fingernails
Pedale (ped.) pedal
percuter to strike
peu a little
piacere pleasure, discretion
più more
pizzicato (pizz.) plucked
plötzlich sudden
plus more
pochissimo very little
poco little
ponticello bridge
portamento (port.) a continuous movement from one pitch to another

precedente preceding
prés close to
presser rush
prima first
quasi almost
que as
ralenti slower
ralentir slowing down
rallentando (rall., rallent) becoming slower
rasch swiftly
rebondir to bounce
recitative (recit.) a singing style imitating speech
retenu held back
revenir return
rhythmisch rhythmic
Rhythmus rhythm
rilassando relaxing
ritardando (rit., ritard) slowing
ritardiert slowed-down
ritenuto (riten.) holding back
roh crude
rosace sound hole (guitar)
rubato with a flexible tempo
Rücksicht regard
ruhig quiet
ruvido rough, coarse
samt including
Saite string
sans without
scherzando playfully
Schlagwerk percussion
schnell fast
schwerer heavier
sehr very
sempre always
senza without
sich Zeit lassen to take time
simile in a similar way
selennemente solemnly
sonorité tone
sopra before, earlier
sordino (sord.) mute
staccato (stacc.) detached
Steg bridge

steigernd   raising, increasing

stringendo   becoming faster

subitement, subito   suddenly

sul   on

sur   on

Takt   measure

taktiren   to beat time

tenero   tender

tenuto (ten.)   sustained

tief   low

Ton   note, tone

touche   fingerboard

tranquilo   tranquil

tremolo (trem.)   rapid reiteration of one or more notes

très   very

trill (tr.), Triller   rapid alternation between two adjacent notes

tutti   all

toujours   always

übergreifen   reach over

übernehmen, übernimmt   to overtake

un   a

una corda   instruction to use the left pedal on the piano; causes hammer to strike a single string for each key

Unterbrechung   interruption

verhaltend   restrained

verklingen   to fade away

vers   toward

vibrato (vib.)   a slight fluctuation of pitch on a sustained note

vibrer   vibrate

vif   lively

vite   fast

vivo   lively

Viertel   quarter note

voce   voice

Vorhang   curtain

vorwärts   forward

wie   like

wieder   again

zart   tender

zu   to

zurückhaltend   holding back